I0830107

Sunshine and Ice
Volume 12

HUMOUR AND MIRACLES

MARTIN MONEY

Published by New Generation Publishing in 2016

Copyright © Martin Money 2016

First Edition

The author asserts the moral right under the Copyright, Designs and Patents Act 1988 to be identified as the author of this work.

All Rights reserved. No part of this publication may be reproduced, stored in a retrieval system or transmitted, in any form or by any means without the prior consent of the author, nor be otherwise circulated in any form of binding or cover other than that which it is published and without a similar condition being imposed on the subsequent purchaser.

www.newgeneration-publishing.com

New Generation Publishing

HUMOUR AND MIRACLES

Part One

January to April 2016

INTRODUCTION – RUTHLESS PEOPLE

I've often referred in my books to ruthless people. By this I mean those horrible articles with ice in their veins that don't care who gets hurt as long as they're okay. They're selfish in the extreme and single-minded in their savagely-hewn intentions.

Unfortunately, they're often in positions of great power, having clawed their way to the top leaving broken and bloody piles of dead or wounded casualties in their wake.

But let's face it; we can all be ruthless, with widely varying degrees of regularity. It can be on purpose or unintentionally – subconsciously even. Sometimes it's necessary for self-preservation. Others it's used for convenience, expediency or clarity.

I have a ruthless streak. Of course I have. I've needed it at times. But it's not a wide one, or at least I don't think it is. I certainly hope not. And I fully accept that what I see as my occasional lack of tact could be taken as indifference, cruelty even.

I'm not alone in that. Each and every one of us has a tendency for ruthlessness. Anybody who denies this is a deluded fool. But some have made careers of it. It's second nature to them. And they're the ones I have a huge problem with.

As I write we're entering 2016 with some very hard-hearted and completely ruthless sods in charge of us. No change there, you might say, but it's the stark realization that the stakes are now so damned high that scares the crap of me I can tell you.

Of course the more cold-bloodedly ruthless among us often use another very effective tool to frequently devastating effect – mind manipulation.

Let's be honest – we all play mind games with each other, all the time – mostly without meaning to. We all like to get our own way and it's a normal, natural human instinct to try and exercise a certain amount of control over our lives.

The alternative of feeling powerless and vulnerable is a pretty frightening prospect.

But some vicious individuals deliberately and constantly mess with others' heads in a callous and selfish quest to always be on top, making others dance to their tunes. And that's when it gets dark and nasty, ugly and intolerable.

Unfortunately, a mile-wide ruthless streak is often accompanied by a zealous impulse to control and manipulate. This applies to so-called ordinary people as well as, more worryingly, our uncaring overlords.

But enough of the heavy stuff – on to lighter things.

Here I go, starting another book as I approach my 62nd birthday next month. I have my lovely family, my brilliant friends and my treasured Paula to keep me occupied and happy and prevent me cracking up or giving up.

Here comes *Sunshine and Ice, Volume Twelve*. I hope you like it…

CHAPTER ONE – LEGENDS AND LOSS

January 7 – Well, 2016 starts with a sad anniversary. It's exactly one year on from the Charlie Hebdo atrocity in Paris. And during those 12 months, things have only got worse on the terrorism front with violent, lethal attacks on innocents across the globe.

During the past week we've also learned of the demise of singer Natalie Cole on New Year's Eve from heart failure. She was 65.

Daughter of the legendary crooner Nat King Cole, Natalie carved a career in her own right as a soul and r'n'b star, songwriter and actress.

Death and destruction is just as widespread as ever, it seems. But there's joy, too.

I'm pleased as punch to be starting 2016 with my precious Paula by my side. Well, I say by my side but that's in the emotional and spiritual sense rather than the physical. I haven't seen her since early on January 2 – only five days but it seems like an age.

We miss each other like crazy when we're apart so we make the most of every moment we're together. And we're in daily contact on Facebook.

In truth I've deeply loved that woman for years and I've fallen in love with her all over again since we became reunited last summer. I love her more than ever.

January 8 – Happy 69th birthday David Bowie. In an age when words like genius, icon and legend are criminally over-used, the Thin White Duke is among the very few people truly deserving such accolades.

He helped change the face of music and he's right up there with the likes of John Lennon, Kate Bush, Jimi Hendrix and Bob Marley. Yeah – that good!

January 11 – Bloody Hell – and he's gone! I switched on the telly news today to learn with shock and horror that Bowie has died after an 18-month battle with cancer he'd kept top secret. He was only 69 but a heavy smoker for most of his adult life.

Facebook is predictably and quite rightly going crazy. This is a massive loss to the entertainment world that cannot possibly be underestimated.

Born David Jones in Brixton, London on 8 January 1947, he shot to fame in the early 1970s playing the part of his alter-ego alien rock star persona Ziggy Stardust, performing an album and tour under that name.

But he never stayed in one place for long and went through a series of ch-ch-changes, constantly re-inventing himself and his music through glam, rock, electronic and soul.

He was a brave pioneer – a cross-dresser with a blurred gender identity when it was still very much taboo. He even appeared on one album cover wearing a dress.

He was also an actor and painter. And he was universally loved and respected.

RIP David – and thanks for sharing your amazing talent with us mere mortals.

Good grief – Lemmy now Bowie. This is a terrible time for music and especially for people of my age group, seeing our heroes pass away with alarming frequency.

It certainly makes us acutely aware of our own mortality and the fact that time is running out for us as well. I'm stunned and numb – and in tears.

I was playing Bowie CDs the other day – his birthday. Now I'm going to play some more. Lots more. His music will live forever.

The passing of Lemmy and then him in such quick succession has been a double whammy for me. I have rarely been so emotionally devastated by the demise of a pop star – or in this case, two.

The last time I was this traumatised and teary-eyed at the loss of a musical icon was when George Harrison shuffled off this mortal coil in 2001. Before that it was John Lennon's sudden departure in 1980 – made more shocking because he was murdered.

Yes, I was saddened and moved when Amy Winehouse, Jimi Hendrix, Brian Jones, Phil Lynott, Jim Morrison, Keith Moon, Bob Marley, Freddie Mercury, Paul Kossoff, Cilla Black, John Bonham, Kurt Cobain, Joe Cocker and others went to the other side.

And Rick Mayall, Peter Cook, Dudley Moore, Kenny Everett, Ronnie Barker, Spike Milligan, Tony Hancock, Eric Morcambe and Ernie Wise.

I was in bits when George Best popped his boots.

But in these four cases – the two ex-Beatles, Lemmy and David – I've been hit especially hard. This is massive and important – to me and the rest of the world.

No wonder I've been sobbing like a softie this morning watching the bulletins, film footage and tributes on the BBC News channel.

Those a bit older than me probably felt much the same when Elvis left the building. Or Sinatra. Or Marilyn Monroe.

It goes without saying that I'm merely speaking of famous people here. When it comes to family and close pals, the pain and tears are far more profound and private, rarely shared with outsiders – unless the recently deceased is well-known of course.

In complete contrast and on a far happier note, it's my grandson Harvey's 5th birthday today. Happy birthday young man, have a fantastic time!

January 13 – Went for my first stroll of the year through Fisherman's Walk to the cliff top and back this morning. It was sunny with a blue sky but the air was a bit crisp, which you expect at this time of year.

But then, we've been so spoiled lately with one of the warmest, mildest winters on record.

As usual, I sat for a while on a bench overlooking the sea, contemplating life and its peculiar twist and turns.

January 15 – Accomplished actor Alan Rickman has died at the age of 69. Cause? – Need you ask? – the dreaded big C again!

Frigging Hell – It's a bleeding epidemic! The sooner we can find a cure for this evil, lethal disease the better. Humanity's arch enemy is claiming far too many people and taking them from us years before their time. It's horrible and tragic.

Come on scientists! – You can work out how to send rockets into space, connect us with each other across the globe through the internet and mobile phones and do tricky, life saving brain and open heart surgery. Surely we're close to finding a cure now?

London-born Alan Rickman was a highly skilled and successful Shakespearean actor who played many varied parts but became especially known as a baddie in blockbuster movies like *Harry Potter*, *Robin Hood Prince of Thieves* and *Die Hard*.

He was also one of the stars of the romantic comedy *Love Actually* alongside Hugh Grant, Colin Firth, Keira Knightley and Emma Thompson.

Now that's a film I love, actually. My very good friend Kerry Smith first suggested I check it out; pretty sure I'd thoroughly enjoy it. Thanks Kez – you were spot on.

Just like *Coyote Ugly*, also quite rightly recommended to me by my close mate Sam (as in Samantha) Excell, *Love Actually* is often perceived as a soppy "chick flick" to be avoided by blokes at all costs.

But my closest female friends know I'd rather watch a well-crafted, well-acted and witty-scripted romantic tale or comedy than some brainless, tedious, violent action extravaganza with muscles, fast cars and explosions but bog all in the way of plot.

(For action with intelligence see the superb Bond, Terminator and Matrix sets.)

Oh, and talking of love, I was thinking about that very topic a little earlier today.

I was especially pondering the fact that, for me, love-making should be sweet and beautiful and romantic, not wild, unfettered and animalistic as some would have it.

Leaving cuts and bruises on someone's body, deep claw marks on their back or knocking their teeth out is not my idea of showing respect, care or affection.

Nah, that just suggests that the person inflicting the injuries is a bit unhinged and prone to violence. Leave the rough stuff to wolves and tigers I say.

I fully accept that all men can act like wolves and all women can resemble tigresses when their loved ones are threatened, particularly their children. That's the way it should be (within reason of course).

But when such basic and brutal behaviour is brought into human coupling, that's when it begins to get dark and twisted.

And if undue pressure or coercion is used, bordering on force, we're starting to enter the realms of sexual assault and ultimately rape.

That's definitely not acceptable in my book. But each to his or her own I suppose.

One of my favourite sayings comes into play here – if everyone in any scenario is happy and they're all clear on the rules, nobody gets seriously or unnecessarily hurt.

January 16 – I have many reasons to love my amazing Paula to the next galaxy and back. She's beautiful – and I don't just mean physically attractive.

Her personality shines like a beacon. She's intelligent, practical, thoughtful, warm, friendly and funny. Her huge heart means that she cares about people – passionately. Even those she's only just met. She's always helping others out, putting them first.

And she makes me feel so flipping good. Younger and more alive, vibrant and confident than I have in years. She says the nicest things to me – about my better qualities and my far from perfect body.

She recently told me that if we were both younger she would have wanted to have my children. Blimey! – That's just about the biggest compliment a woman could possibly pay a man. I was deeply moved, completely blown away. Still am.

And, she is good looking. Her alluring blue eyes with that mischievous sparkle, lush legs and mighty fine figure, combined with her personal charm, make her a real catch.

She could have any bloke she wants so I'm over the moon that she's chosen to be with me. Sometimes I wonder why. I'm so damned lucky.

One of my female friends told me I'm punching way above my weight with Paula so I need to treat her right if I want to keep her. A bit blunt and tactless maybe, but I can see what she meant.

In fact I keep telling myself: "Martin, don't mess it up this time." For to lose Paula again would be a tragedy – especially as we're reunited after all these years apart. My heart would be well and truly broken. I know a good thing when it comes my way.

And when I refer to "my Paula" I'm not meaning it in the weirdly creepy, possessive sense some fellers do. You know the ones – those chauvinistic knob heads who regard women as property like homes, cars or sheds. Or even worse – skivvies.

No, she's mine because she's decided she wants to be. She's very much her own person. I would say ours is an equal partnership, but in truth she's in charge. Always has been, always will be. And I wouldn't have it any other way.

It gives me a great thrill to say "my Paula" – and I hope it conveys in a positive way just how very proud and fortunate I feel that she's picked me as her love interest.

January 17 – I was sat watching an episode of the brilliant historical comedy programme *Blackadder* yesterday and thought: "It's time for another list."

Those who have read my previous books will know I love making lists – especially of my favourites from the arts and entertainment world. It's a very enjoyable way of giving structure to great times spent watching or listening to golden top-notch stuff.

In this case I'm going to be focussing on my top 20 British sitcoms of all time.

The four *Blackadder* series, written by Richard Curtis and Ben Elton and starring Rowan Atkinson, Tony Robinson, Miranda Richardson, Stephen Fry, Hugh Laurie, Patsy Byrne and Tim McInnerny, come in at number three.

Apart from the skilled and hilarious wordplay and script, delivered excellently by a terrific cast, this show had a host of superb guest stars including Peter Cook, Rik Mayall, Ade Edmondson, Robbie Coltrane, Brian Blessed and Miriam Margolyes.

And that is the key to a great sitcom – Good ideas, clever writing and a strong set of characters played by actors at the top of their game. The first great masterpiece in this respect was *Dad's Army*. And all of the programmes in my list fit that bill.

Blackadder is right up there with the very best. That's why it's my number three, only beaten by *Fawlty Towers* – often cited as the finest British sitcom of all – and *Only Fools and Horses*, which narrowly takes the crown due to John Sullivan's genius for mixing comedy and pathos.

Richard Curtis is very much Sullivan's equal here, as evidenced by the films *Love Actually* and *Four Weddings and a Funeral*, but we don't see much of that potent mix in *Blackadder*, which goes full-throttle for laughs except for its outstanding, deeply moving and very memorable final episode.

Anyway, without further ado, here's my top 20:

1, *Only Fools and Horses*; 2, *Fawlty Towers*; 3, *Blackadder*; 4; *Dad's Army*; 5, *Hancock's Half Hour*; 6, *Father Ted*; 7, *Red Dwarf*; 8, *Till Death Us Do Part*; 9, *The Young Ones*; 10, *Two Pints of Lager and a Packet of Crisps*; 11, *The Inbetweeners*, 12, *The Vicar of Dibley*; 13, *Porridge*; 14, *The Good Life*; 15, *Yes Minister*; 16, *One Foot in the Grave*; 17, *Drop the Dead Donkey*; 18, *Birds of a Feather*; 19, *Men Behaving Badly*; 20, *Some Mothers Do 'Ave 'Em*.

Others will have their own opinions and will probably challenge the order or point to what they see as glaring exclusions. *Miranda* immediately springs to mind – not included yet but give it another good series or two and its well on course to make it.

I've thoroughly enjoyed watching that show, as I have many other sitcoms not mentioned above – *Absolutely Fabulous, Keeping up Appearances, The Likely Lads, Hi De Hi, Bread, Waiting for God* and *Last of the Summer Wine* for example.

And other similar shows not classed as sitcoms for some reason, such as *Ideal*.

Other excellent British comedies have included *Monty Python's Flying Circus, Brass Eye, The Office*, the *League of Gentlemen, Nighty Night* and *Fresh Meat*.

My favourite American sitcom ever has to be the sublime *Friends*.

And talking of lists, it occurred to me the other day that the recently-deceased and incredibly talented David Bowie hadn't featured much in my rundowns of my favourite lyricists. This was a bad oversight because he was extremely good.

I've been reminded of this fact on listening again to a lot of his music since his shocking demise a week ago today.

January 19 – And another one bites the dust! Glenn Frey of the Eagles has passed away, aged 67, after battling complications arising from rheumatoid arthritis, colitis and pneumonia.

I really liked the Eagles. I've previously recounted how knocked sideways I was on first hearing their single One of These Nights, which he co-wrote. I thought it was fresh and different and exciting, and I quickly grew to greatly admire their music.

Hotel California, which guitarist Frey also co-wrote, is another brilliant effort, widely regarded as one of the best rock songs ever.

Life in the Fast Lane, Desperado, Lyin' Eyes, Take it to the Limit, New Kid in Town and Take it Easy were other great Eagles tracks Frey had a hand in composing.

The group was one of the biggest rock acts ever, selling more than 150 million records worldwide. And Frey, who sang many of the hits, played a key part.

RIP Glenn, and thanks for the music.

January 20 – Last night I watched a disturbing and frightening Channel Four telly documentary called *The Jihadis Next Door*.

It told of Islamic extremists in London and their hate-fuelled warning that their flag will fly over Downing Street as the world succumbs to Sharia Law – their strict and, according to them, pure version of their faith.

They equate democracy with hypocrisy and see themselves as waging war against their oppressors – led in this country by David Cameron and the UK Government.

And the film showed police trying to combat aggressive confrontations between them and other Muslims who they accuse of betraying Islamic principles but who in turn see them as dishonest and dangerous twisters of their shared religion.

The radicals stopped just short of admitting they were members of, or recruiting for, the dreaded, outlawed Islamic State, which would have risked their being jailed.

But they made it clear that they were working to the same ends – replacement of our current flawed Western system with a strictly-enforced worldwide Islamic regime.

At the other end of the scale (apparently), this morning's TV news had more on Donald Trump, the billionaire American presidential candidate.

He's demanded a "total and complete shutdown" of Muslims entering the US. Our own Parliament is to discuss banning him from the UK for using such hateful rhetoric.

Today's news centred on the fact that fellow Republican and right-wing nut Sarah Palin, who herself ran for vice-president in 2008, is backing Trump.

No surprise there, you might say, but in an equally disturbing and frightening style mirroring the Islamic extremists she spoke of wanting to see Trump as the USA's "commander in chief."

This deliberate choice of phrase carried a crystal clear implication that the USA is similarly in war mode.

Oh, and UK defence minister Michael Fallon today urged that the coalition of countries fighting the so-called Islamic State (IS) network must focus on a "tightening of the noose" around its Syrian heartlands.

He said this at a meeting in Paris also involving his counterparts from Germany, France and America.

So the sabre-rattling rhetoric continues unabated as the fierce and deadly ideological war intensifies from both sides. It scares me greatly.

I used the word "apparently" a few paragraphs back for a very good reason, for, as I've previously stated, I see political ideas forming a circle, not a straight line, and I find all intolerant, extremist words and actions as equally abhorrent.

January 21 – I'm stunned, mortified, gutted and any other words you could use to describe acute distress. Paula's ended our relationship.

We love each other very deeply and will always be the best of pals, there for each other, caring and concerned. But the couple bit is over.

The year 2016 is turning into a bitch all round – what with Lemmy, Bowie, disaster, misery and death at home and abroad, the worsening international crisis threatening us all and now this.

There have been cracks in our relationship for a while, if the truth be told. I just didn't realize it had got this bad.

Paula and I will stay the closest of mates, that's guaranteed. It just means the terms of our interaction have been redefined – returned to what they were previously.

And, whatever happens now, she's given me the best six months I've had for nearly 20 years, made me happier than I ever thought I could possibly be again, boosted my confidence no end and made me dream once more. I'm forever in her debt for that.

I'm hurting like hell right now but I'll get over it. If my life's dramatic twists and turns have taught me anything it's that I'm a survivor – like Paula. We'll both be fine.

January 22 – Wishing a very happy birthday to my good friend John Gaynor. Have a memorable one, mate!

I've just had a thought. If you have to fight to win someone back, they clearly don't think enough of you to warrant it.

January 23 – And more bad news. Very bad indeed. I switched on my computer this morning and went on to Facebook to find a private message from my old mucker Kerry Smith telling me our great friend Theresa Bevis had passed away, aged just 50.

Dear Theresa's had health problems for a few years now and wasn't a well bunny, but this is still a massive shock. She had a cardiac arrest brought on by an asthma attack.

To say we were best mates is putting it mildly. I once wrote that Theresa and I were as close as two people could possibly be without being an item. Kerry liked that.

But in all honesty I think special friendships like ours can be deeper and more lasting than so-called relationships anyway.

It's the same or similar with Kerry, Shaz, Carole, Christine, Sam, Jen Clough, Bev Jones, Michelle Adye, Claire Kimber, Tina Wilkins and Paula, although in her case we recently tried the couple bit and it didn't work out.

Lovers come and go but a true best friend is for keeps. Some lucky souls have both in the same person – my parents did and so have my son Phil and his wife Emily.

I have many fond memories of my times with Theresa and numerous humorous stories I could tell, some of them printable. I recounted one of them in an earlier book – in edited form of course. She was a lovely lady, a true pal.

I'm devastated and teary-eyed – and many others will be too. Kerry and Paula for starters. We all loved our Theresa.

And poor John would have heard about it on his birthday. I wrote a few paragraphs ago that I wanted it to be a memorable one for him. Careful what you wish for, eh?

We all feel for Theresa's family, and especially her three children (well, I say children but they're all grown up now). Her twin sister Samantha died a few years back.

Farewell favourite friend. Rest in Peace sweetie. You were a beautiful person, a first-class pal and drinking buddy. I've lit a candle and I'm dedicating this book to you.

Gordon bleedin' Bennett – 2016 was already becoming a crap year but it seems to be getting worse by the day. And it's still only sodding January!

January 23, several hours later – What do you do when you feel like your life's unravelling and it's all starting to look more than a little bleak and hopeless? In my case, it's one of two things.

I either go for a walk through woodland to the nearby cliff top to sit looking at the sea and beautiful vistas of the Dorset coastline – or I immerse myself in my beloved music. I find both extremely therapeutic.

For the past few days I've been doing the latter quite a lot, playing back to back David Bowie and Motorhead CDs. I've just watched *Lemmy the Movie* on catch-up TV and after writing this brief journal entry I'm going to play it again, it's that flipping good.

Because when it comes to music, nothing lifts the spirits more than an invigorating injection of good old life-affirming rock and roll. And if you're talking the straight down the line, no frills variety, no-one's done it better than Lemmy and Motorhead.

AC/DC have done it just as well but nobody's done it better.

Problems, hassle and hurt don't miraculously vanish, but the music and short trips to the sea front always work wonders in reviving my faith in the better aspects of human existence.

January 24 – People are in your life for a reason – but not always the one you think.

As I write, I'm playing the Motorhead album Bomber. In all the talk of this band being the loudest in the world and Lemmy being a larger-than-life, hard rocking folk hero, it's often forgotten, or at least overlooked, just how good a songwriter he was.

Buried beneath the intense volume, rasping vocals, manic bass lines and aggressive posturing are some mighty fine tunes with skilful, potent and intelligent lyrics.

And, having met and chatted with him, I can testify that behind the gruff exterior was a very pleasant and friendly bloke – a regular guy with no rock star pretensions at all.

I said in a previous book that my generation grew up with rock music and it was so deeply ingrained in our culture and experiences that ours became rock and roll lives.

This applied whether we were well-known or not, overt rebels or just playing along with a dreadful system we despised in order to make ends meet.

But we've all accepted that living a rock and roll lifestyle – even a relatively tame form of it like mine – with all the alcohol, smoking, partying and other factors involved, has carried certain health risks. Actions have consequences.

Theresa knew that. So did Andy, Umo, Celtic Nicky, Hairy Pete, Lee and Canadian Mike. So do Sam, Paula and other mates of mine. I do, and so did David Bowie and Lemmy – although in their cases they did take it all to further extremes than most.

That's why so many people around my age, both friends and famous, are now passing away so young. Disease has claimed most of them, but the lifestyle hasn't helped.

Would any of us have had it otherwise? What do you think?

That said, in my case the heart crisis forced me to re-evaluate and – perhaps belatedly – take steps to try and ensure I'll stick around for as long as possible.

I've given up smoking and more closely watch my alcohol, fat, sugar and salt intakes.

I eat more vegetables, less red meat, have a daily glass of fruit juice, observe a healthier diet and do more exercise but I'm still taking certain risks, fully aware of what I'm doing, because I refuse to live like a monk and want to continue having fun.

You can't stop the ageing process or control when you fall ill and pass away, but you can try to delay it. Too much damage might already have been done and I've had to face the fact that I'm in my twilight years, but I'm in no dashing hurry to go just yet.

January 25 – Paula's recent decision to end us as a couple hit me like a truck. Theresa's demise so soon afterwards hit me like a bigger one. My heart was broken twice within three days.

I'm still reeling, but I'm now coming to terms with both eventualities. I'll be okay.

And with Paula the most important thing is we're still the best of friends. To lose her in that capacity now, having finally got her back in my life after almost two decades, would have been a much too high a price to pay for six wonderful months as her man.

As the dust from the debris settles, I can see more clearly the parallels between my friendship with Paula and the one I had with Theresa, who I knew for even longer.

Of course, the significant difference is that Paula and I recently tried being an item – well, sort of. Theresa and I never did. But in many ways we were closer than that.

I have several really close female pals. But I don't as a rule kiss them on the lips. I have Paula, even when we we've not been a couple. And I did Theresa – her idea.

And when we walked somewhere together, Theresa would hold on to my arm. Okay, sometimes it was to help steady herself when she'd had too many vodkas, but it was still really nice. So was the lip kissing. That was how we were. It was beautiful.

Paula also loved Theresa and she's as cut up about our dear friend's demise as I am. We'll raise a glass or two to her when we meet up tomorrow at the Bell – scene of so many classic Theresa moments.

Golden memories of my times with Theresa have flooded back over the past two days. Kerry and Paula have been similarly

17

reminiscing with tear stained eyes. And a lot of others too –
Theresa was a very popular, extremely highly regarded lady.

January 26 – I've had a great adventure during the last six months
or so – a proper thrill ride.

It's been an exciting and invigorating excursion into the outside
world of adult issues and raw emotion – pleasure and pain mixed
in a potent, fizzing cocktail. I've felt alive.

But the adventure has shuddered to an abrupt halt, the wheels have
come off and the dream is over. It's time to retreat back into my
shell, marvelling at my recent good fortune but also licking my
wounds.

It's cosy, warm and safe here. I feel out of harm's way, like I can
avoid getting further hurt. But it is a bit lonely.

****

CHAPTER TWO – HARSH LESSONS

January 27 – Paula and I met up yesterday for a couple of bevvies in the Bell, the first time we'd seen each other face to face since our "split."

It started a tad uncomfortable as we sorted out a few practical details that urgently needed addressing, but that didn't last long at all and very soon we were back to being us again – relaxed, even having a laugh or two.

Our session was indeed tinged with a profound sadness – more a reaction to Theresa's shocking demise than our own situation. But it was a very pleasant one all the same, the way it should be between us. The way it always has been and will forever remain.

Recovering from a relationship breakdown is a bit like mourning. But the loss of our great friend has put it all into perspective for us both. And I don't see our "break up" that dramatically anyway – as I said, we've redefined the terms of our link, that's all.

There's been no massive falling out and there will be no bitterness or recriminations (although there have been tears). I think it's horrible when couples part acrimoniously – it's a traumatic enough time without all that nonsense.

Paula and I are just fine – always will be. Our closest of friendships is built on the sturdiest of foundations – honesty, trust, mutual respect and deep affection on both sides. We're soul mates who love each other very much but we're no longer in love.

Relationships come in many forms and ours is strong – unbreakable, in fact.

And I would add that in my eyes our special friendship has just passed the ultimate acid test – and with flying colours I reckon.

January 28 – Happy birthday to my nephew, Jonathan.

It really riles me when people talk about someone being a typical man or typical woman, especially when the comment is aimed in my direction.

I mean what the Hell does that mean? We're all individuals for goodness sake – each one of us a unique expression of an aspect of the Whole.

The only typical I am is a typical Martin Money because there is only one of me (some might say thank the stars for that). Even twins have different personalities.

I accept that in the broadest terms possible a male perspective on the world may be different from a female one in certain respects. But I hate sweeping generalisations.

And, as I've said before – probably more than once – I see the whole battle of the sexes garbage as a waste of time, at best inane and at worst unnecessarily corrosive.

Let's face it, if you said someone was a typical German, Asian or Jew, that would be quite rightly perceived as a racist slur or unacceptable religious or ethnic insult.

So why is referring to a typical woman not regarded as blatant sexism? And what on Earth is a typical academic, manual worker, tenant or toff? Careless labels anger me.

January 29 – Human existence is a learning curve, so they say. And it's just taught Paula and me two harsh lessons in one hit – to our great regret.

The first was that you should never start a romantic, sexual relationship on the rebound – it's doomed to failure and will end in tears for both of you.

Lesson two was that two good pals shouldn't try to be an item, for the same reasons.

In our case, we're very fortunate that our close bond is that strong that it's survived and we've been able to revert to our former status relatively quickly and smoothly.

It's been a very tough week for both of us, made worse by Theresa's passing, but we're okay now. We're cool.

Life is full of broken promises and shattered dreams. But it's also jam-packed with love and joy, humour and miracles.

Hey, the cynical optimist rides again!

January 30 – Yesterday (Friday) evening was a good one. Sam invited me to hers for a booze and fun session – and it was just what I needed to lift my spirits from the pain and sadness I've suffered of late.

It was especially nice when my other great friend Kerry Smith turned up to join us and I had a chance to talk to her face-to-face about Theresa and her funeral next Thursday (February 4).

Apart from Sam, Carl, Kerry and me, others there for all or part of the proceedings were Tina Mcauley, Jem Hannen, Rich Jeffery, Russell Hall and a guy called Jimmy.

Sam, Tina and Kerry were especially supportive towards me and it was great to be with good mates and actually manage to have a laugh. Everything seemed brighter and more normal again.

January 31 – Veteran BBC broadcaster Sir Terry Wogan has died of cancer, aged 77.

Born in Limerick, Ireland on 3 August 1938, he passed away earlier today after a short battle with the illness.

He became a family favourite for millions during a 50-year career that included a radio breakfast show and hit TV programmes such as *Eurovision, Blankety Blank,* the annual *Children in Need* charity appeal and a three times a week chat show.

His stature in the entertainment world was so huge he certainly deserves a mention. But I didn't really like him that much so I'll leave it at that.

February 1 – Had a good night at the Bell yesterday (Sunday), that was just as therapeutic as Friday was round Sam and Carl's.

I had a few drinks with friends including John Palmer, John Gaynor, Ben Avill, Jenny Daniels, Mark Evans, Laura Williams, Simon "Squeak" Turnbull and Matt Brant, who was especially caring and supportive and displayed great wisdom. Cheers mate!

February 2 – I've been writing another lyric during the past two days. Here it is:

***Stilettos*, Martin Money**
Jan 31–Feb 2, 2016

Another spin on the roller coaster took my breath away
I'm stunned and bruised, I'm cut and lost and almost rued the day
I first met you, I love you so and that will never change
It's us forever though you've felt the urge to re-arrange

Another year on this crazy planet, new man in your life
A fresher source of hope and dreams to ease the hurt and strife
Another cause of joy and tears to meddle with your head
It's tough to grasp the fact he's now a feature in your bed

And every time you say his name it chills me to the bone
Stilettos pierce my wounded heart; I'm feeling so alone,
Yeah, so alone

Another fail in the sphere of romance rocks my world again
And here I am once more, a scarred survivor of the pain
I'm old enough for sure but lack the wisdom of my peers
I guess that's just the way it is, the path I've trod for years

It was brilliant but it's over now – it was dreamlike but not true
And though we're not together there will still be me and you
But every time you say his name it chills me to the bone
Stilettos pierce my wounded heart; I'm feeling so alone
Yeah, so alone

You're my best friend, my soul mate and that will have no end
Even though you've felt the need to sever ties and not pretend
You're a ray of light, you're beautiful and close we'll always be
I only want the best for you; you feel the same for me

Another spin on the roller coaster took my breath away
I'm stunned and bruised, I'm cut and lost and almost rued the day
I first met you, I love you so and that will never change
It's us forever though you've felt the urge to re-arrange

Another year on this crazy planet, new man in your life
A fresher source of hope and dreams to ease the hurt and strife
Another cause of joy and tears to meddle with your head
It's tough to grasp the fact he's now a feature in your bed

And every time you say his name it chills me to the bone
Stilettos pierce my wounded heart; I'm feeling so alone
Yeah, so alone.

February 5 – Yesterday was tough. We attended Theresa's funeral. And when I say we, I mean myself, Kerry Smith, (who kindly drove me about), Paula Carruthers, Debi Browning, Alan Painter, Dave Perry, Steve Elvidge and Maria Harris.

The service, at Bournemouth Crematorium was packed – standing room only – because Theresa was a lovely, popular lady with many friends.

That was followed by a wake at the Bevis family home in Keeble Road in the town's northern sector, hosted by Theresa's three grown-up children Ryan, Chloe and Jack.

From there, Kerry, Maria, Debs, Al, Paula and I went on to the Bell for a few drinks. It had to be done, for that pub was Theresa's local too for many years before she moved out of Boscombe.

We met Tina and Jeff McNally there and other pub regulars and ended up taking part in the weekly Thursday evening quiz – just as Theresa, Kerry and me used to as a trio.

Back then we called ourselves the Wobbly Heads – our slang term for a strong German lager with an unpronounceable name – and we revived the moniker yesterday evening, for one night only, in our great mate's honour.

We came third and Kerry gave the quizmaster a hard time – just as Theresa often did. It was a good send off – friends joining together in memory of one of our number sadly no longer physically with us. We even laughed a few times amid the tears.

Theresa would have liked that and in fact wanted it – she was a fun-loving girl who had asked that people wore something red for the day, her favourite colour.

As I said a few pages back, we all loved our Theresa. And we'll all miss her terribly.

Talking about people passing away, two more famous figures in the entertainment world have gone – actor Frank Finlay and singer-songwriter Maurice White.

Finlay, 89, was a stage and screen veteran who played a variety of roles from Iago opposite Laurence Olivier's Othello to Porthos in the comedy adventure films *The Three Musketeers* and *The Four Musketeers*.

He died of heart failure after a long illness.

White, 74, was the founder of soul group Earth, Wind & Fire, who had a string of hits including September, Boogie Wonderland, Shining Star and After the Love has Gone.

He was diagnosed with Parkinson's disease in 1992 and his condition was reported to have got worse in recent months.

February 9 – Wishing a very happy birthday to Rachel Cooper (Emily's sister) and also my friend Mark "Tich" Hemington. Hope they both have good ones!

Oh, and belated birthday greetings go out to Matt Brant (February 6) and Ollie Okoye (February 7).

I've already mentioned that Matt has been particularly supportive during my Paula and Theresa low period. So have Sam, Tina Mcauley, Kerry and other mates.

In fact, I told Kerry I couldn't have handled last Thursday, the day of Theresa's funeral, without her by my side. She said she felt the same.

The past two weeks or so have been a torrid time for me but I'm now emerging from the gloom and seeing things in sharper focus – getting my perspective back.

People have seen me laughing and apparently having a good time more than once during the fortnight, thanks to the healthy influence of mates' company and support.

Plus, as I've explained before more than once, my sense of humour goes up a couple of gears when crisis strikes – it's a highly effective defence mechanism. But the smiles are forced, the laughter hollow.

When I've been home alone – yeah, that's when the devastating effects have really hit me. I've shed most of my tears in private.

More song words have popped into my head as I've tried to come to terms with it all. Here they are:

Bournemouth's Sheba Queen, **Martin Money**
February 2-9, 2016

She was beautiful in the finest sense, a friend for life indeed
But now she's gone and far too fast our broken hearts all bleed
Her air of fun, her wicked smile and sense of mischief strong
Her kindness, care and loyalty, her passion for a song

She was a star, our dearest lass, Bournemouth's Sheba Queen
Lovely but formidable, fierce but never mean
Fair and decent, treasured pal who warmed us to the core
Her spirit lives in all of us and will for evermore

You made us smile and lit our lives so each one seemed less rotten
Theresa, Theresa, you'll never be forgotten

Adored by friends and family, devoted to her dogs
She relished simple honesty and shunned all "clever clogs"
She hated falsehood, those in masks or with an extra face
And since she passed away the world's become a colder place
You made us smile and lit our lives so each one seemed less rotten
Theresa, Theresa, you'll never be forgotten.

Time to Pretend, Martin Money
February 8-9, 2016

Brutal rejection, smashed up dreams
Savaged affection, shattered schemes
Saw my hopes come crashing down
Felt my smile turn to a frown
Felt my laughter change to tears
Heart all broken, realized fears
Found in time then snatched from me –
Happy ending couldn't be

Time to pretend that I'm okay
Forcing the laughter ev'ry day
While inside I scream silently
As my soul yearns and burns for you

Stunned by surprise and disbelief
Gunned down by lies and stabbed by grief
Cut adrift and on my own
Once again I'm so alone
Watched my ideals melt away
Thought this one had come to stay
Love and comfort here at last
Then I felt that ice cold blast

Time to pretend that I'm okay
Forcing the laughter ev'ry day
While inside I scream silently
As my soul yearns and burns for you.

I find that writing lyrics is an excellent and relatively harmless way
of getting deep hurt, anger and bitterness out of my system. It's
also a great vehicle to express my joy when good things happen.

On a happier note, it's Shrove Tuesday today so that means pancakes for tea.

February 10 – And another set of song words, fresh off the press of my mind:

***Used and Abused*, Martin Money**
February 10, 2016

Feeling used, abused, promised then refused
Treated like a king, hung out to dry
He was pleased, at ease then dragged to his knees
Passing sun gave way to stormy sky

He was lost, counting cost, giving in to the frost
When you came his way suddenly
He felt sweet, complete – once more back on his feet
It was all snatched away rapidly

Have you any idea of the damage you've done?
His heart's ripped to shreds, black and blue
How can you move on with you life so damned fast?
He can't do the same without you

He felt bliss with each kiss, a joy he'd long time missed
And thought it was real, here to stay
He had dreams and schemes, felt the finest of serenes
Big smiles turned to tears within a day

Have you any idea of the damage you've done?
His heart's ripped to shreds, black and blue
How can you move on with you life so damned fast?
He can't do the same without you

Feeling used, abused, promised then refused
Treated like a king, hung out to dry
He was pleased, at ease then dragged to his knees
Passing sun gave way to stormy sky

He was lost, counting cost, giving in to the frost
When you came his way suddenly
He felt sweet, complete – once more back on his feet
It was all snatched away brutally

Have you any idea of the damage you've done?
His heart's ripped to shreds, black and blue
How can you move on with you life so damned fast?
He can't do the same without you.

February 11 – And another! Blimey, I'm having a bit of a purple patch lyrically!

Zak's Capture, Martin Money, February 10-11, 2016

Zak was a believer who met a deceiver and fell for her charms and
*   her lies*
Her smile was magnetic, his capture pathetic, those sapphire blue
*   eyes mesmerize*

She made him feel special, just like precious metal; she took him to
*   Heaven then Hell*
No longer a thinker, hers hook, line and sinker, a victim of love's
*   wicked spell*

Zak's so numb and dazed, broken, lost and fazed
He's shifted to a darker point of view
The dream he had was too good to be true

Our crestfallen hero's become a big zero, least that's how he sees
*   himself now*
Was walking on sunshine, she fed him a false line and watched him
*   unravel and how*

She moved like a fast knife, new lover in her life as Zak's broken
*   heart ached and bled*
He'd seen a bright future built with and beside her but now he just
*   can't look ahead*

Zak's so numb and dazed, broken, lost and fazed
He's shifted to a darker point of view
The dream he had was too good to be true

He was a believer who met a deceiver and fell for her charms and
*   her lies*
Her smile was magnetic, his capture pathetic, those sapphire blue
*   eyes hypnotize*

*She moved like a fast knife, new lover in her life as Zak's broken
   heart ached and bled
He'd seen a bright future built with and beside her but now he just
   can't look ahead.*

February 14 – Happy Valentine's Day. Yeah right! – The greeting
has a hollow and bitter ring to it now. It should have been so
different, so nice, so much better. A month ago I was really
looking forward to today. Oh well, shit happens I suppose.

Thank goodness for yesterday, a complete contrast. I had a great
time and it did me a power of good. I got a taxi to Wimborne to
attend Lily's second birthday party. Lily is my grandchildren's
cousin, daughter of Rachel Cooper, Emily's sister.

It was also Ali Quilter's birthday, Ali being my son Phil's
stepsister. She was at Lily's party alongside Phil, Emily, my
grandchildren Chloe and Harvey, Emily's parents Gail and Keith,
Rachel and Em's brother Simon, Phil's mum Joe and others.

After that, Phil and Emily took me back to their place in Ferndown
for a while where I met their new dog Lola, a soppy lurcher puppy,
and chilled playing games with the kids. Phil then kindly gave me
a lift home to save me forking out for another cab.

And at the end of the day, that's what it's all about, isn't it? –
spending highly enjoyable quality time with loved ones. Sod all
that romantic nonsense with its emotional turmoil and heartbreak.
Who needs it?

Oh, by the way, Friday (two days ago) I went round Sam and
Carl's for another booze and fun session that similarly revived my
battered spirits. Its family and mates who keep me going when
things look bleak in this troubled and insane existence.

February 19 – Heartbreak, misery, hassle, tragedy, injury and
death continue to rock our world as politicians and power brokers
persist in ruthlessly playing with our lives.

Methinks it's time to talk books and music.

I've recently finished reading Russell Brand's autobiographical *My Bookie Wook* – a brutally honest but very funny account of his life, including his addictions to drugs, booze and sex.

Many people don't like him but he makes some excellent points about society and he has a brilliant way with words. I thoroughly enjoyed reading the paperback, bought with a W H Smiths voucher – a Christmas present from my nephew Scott and family.

Now I'm two-thirds of the way through Dan Brown's thriller *Digital Fortress*, picked up in a charity shop. He really is a terrific spinner of fast-paced stories about intriguing issues – he also wrote *Angels and Demons* and the *Da Vinci Code*.

Next I'm going to read my hardback copy of his work called *The Lost Symbol*, bought from a different charity shop a few minutes later. It's another of his novels tackling the shady world of secret societies and hidden but vital messages. Superb!

Turning to sounds, I've recently been playing a right old mishmash, as usual, including the Waterboys, the Stranglers, the Who, Bob Marley and Al Stewart.

Although born in Glasgow, singer-songwriter Stewart is regarded as very much a local lad, having grown up in Wimborne, Dorset, 11 miles from Bournemouth.

Most people know him for his classic song the Year of the Cat, which is pretty typical of his mesmerising brand of folk-rock that marries intoxicatingly catchy melodies with a wonderful skill for word-weaving – always a turn on for a lyric writer like me.

February 22 – It's Monday and I've had another very pleasant weekend. Friday I went to Sam's for drinkies and laughs with her, Carl, Tina Mcauley and Rich Jeffery.

Saturday was a quiet one but yesterday evening I ventured to the Bell for a few pints with John Gaynor, Matt Brant, Nicola Williams, Sam Rose Lowney, Mark Evans, Laura Williams, deejay Ross Maslin, Gemma Whike, Clare Hayes and her man Darryl Yarwood – my very good pal Steve's son.

Jem Hannen, another of my closest male buddies, arrived later with his brother Steve, who was celebrating his 61st birthday, so I had a drink with them before leaving.

All in all, another good three days in the life of your mildly unbalanced narrator.

In the outside world, today's news is full of this summer's in-out referendum over Europe. I've said it before and I'll say it again – to leave now would be a disaster for our beleaguered nation.

It's too late – we should have done this 30 years ago, before we got hopelessly entangled in the bureaucratic and legal spider's web of the European super state.

All we can hope to do now is stay in and try to reform it from the inside, halting the relentless advance of the all-powerful European Union juggernaut while sticking up for ourselves as we should have done way back then.

While typing this on my computer keyboard, I'm listening to the sublime music of the mighty fine reggae band Dubheart on CD. Yesterday I was playing Rod Stewart and the Faces. Eclectic, ain't I?

February 24 – Today's a Wednesday so yesterday being Paula's usual day off work; we met at the Bell for a few lagers and a catch-up.

We've decided to see each other once a month or so from now on – as buddies.

I called yesterday's rendezvous early birthday drinks as tomorrow is my 62nd. It was nice to chat to my long-time best pal and hear her news, especially of her recent trip back home to Carlisle to see her son Matt, his lady Emma and their two little girls.

It was the first time Paula had met her second granddaughter, Mattea, born in November, and she was over the moon to do so. On the way back to Bournemouth, she stopped off to see her sister Melanie and family at Bicester.

By all accounts Paula relished seeing her folks again – and I very much liked hearing about it. It's nice to know that friends have had fun lapping up life's better moments.

But I must admit it did hurt – more than a bit – every time she referred to her new man, Mark who drinks in the Cricketers. Oh well, I guess I'll just have to grin and bear it. As long as he treats her right and makes her happy.

Guv'nor Mark Evans mingled with the punters while his equally likable lady and co-manager Laura Williams and lovely barmaid Nicola Williams (no relation) served us our beverages. Others present included Matt Brant, John Palmer and Billy Clarkson.

It was another highly enjoyable session at my local pub.

February 25 – Happy birthday to me and also the late, great George Harrison, who would have been 73. We still miss you loads George, and your best pal John Lennon.

I've lit a candle and I'm playing a Harrison CD as I write. George was spiritual and astute, a superb singer/songwriter/guitarist equally as good as Lennon or McCartney.

For my money, the plural of genius is Beatles. Wise, funny men, brilliant musicians.

And speaking of musicians, yesterday evening's telly was dominated by coverage of the annual Brits awards ceremony, broadcast live from London's O2 Arena.

The night belonged to the excellent Adele, who picked up four statuettes – including the major ones for best British female solo artist; single (Hello) and album (25).

But the icing on the cake was a satellite link up on a massive TV screen featuring astronaut Major Tim Peake, live from the international space station, who reduced the London-born singer to tears in announcing she'd won the Brits global success award.

Coldplay were named best British group, the intriguing Catfish and the Bottlemen best breakthrough act and James Bay somehow picked up the British solo male title while the equally dreadful One Direction inconceivably won the video artists award.

Canadian superstar Justin Bieber was predictably international male solo artist while the decidedly weird Icelandic singer Bjork interestingly won the corresponding female award. Aussie rockers Tame Impala were named best global group.

Barbadian singer/songwriter Rihanna put on a flashy show during which she duetted and gyrated with Canadian rapper Drake. Others performing live included Bieber, vocalists and guitarist Bay and the UK girl group, TV talent show stars Little Mix.

Coldplay opened the proceedings and Adele closed them – the best two acts in my view apart from New Zealand's female rock performer Lorde, who did a terrific David Bowie tribute set alongside the recently-deceased legend's own backing band.

Lorde's music dovetailed nicely with touching eulogies to Bowie from singer Annie Lennox and actor Gary Oldman, a close personal friend of the iconic trailblazer.

The audience, packed with musicians, gave an emotional standing ovation – and quite rightly so. Just like the Beatles, Bowie was also a genius.

Turning to a very serious, worrying matter, my birthday card from my cousin Sandra contained a short hand-written letter in which she informed me she had cancer of the lung, rib and neck and was going to hospital to discuss chemo and radio therapy.

I've written and posted a reply letter sending my best wishes for successful treatment and a fast recovery. But my heart aches for her – she must be scared stiff. I would be.

February 28 – Happy birthday fellow Pisceans John "Brun" Smith and Gary "Gadget" Preston. And I should really extend belated greetings to another pal, Alan Painter, whose personal anniversary was last Saturday, the 20th.

Better late than never, eh Al? – And I did post a Facebook message to him on the actual day.

It's Sunday and speaking for myself I've had a highly enjoyable birthday weekend.

My great mate Sam Excell wasn't well so had to call off the little party she'd planned to throw for me at her home in Roberts Road on Friday.

At a loose end, and having stayed in on my birthday the previous day, I strolled to the Bell, where managers Laura Williams and Mark Evans had kindly put three pints of Fosters lager in behind the bar for me, bless them. Thanks guys, much appreciated!

Jeff and Tina McNally were there, along with John Gaynor, Sam Rose Lowney, Nicola Williams, her mum Penny Williams and Penny's pal Dawn Lewis.

Nicola, a Bell barmaid, had the night off but was in the pub having a drink with her feller. Penny sometimes serves me in Southbourne Nationwide Building Society, where I have an account, and Dawn works at the local One Stop shop I frequent.

Dawn, John and the McNallys were among more than 50 Facebook friends who had sent me happy birthday messages – a huge response that totally blew me away. Some of them were really sweet. I feel blessed to have so many caring chums.

Oh, and Jeff bought me a drink as we chatted. Cheers mate!

Yesterday I had a lovely family day with Phil, Emily, Chloe and Harvey. They gave me two cards – one from the married couple and the other from my three precious grandchildren (Chloe, Harvey and Lucas, not present yesterday).

They also gave me a "best of David Bowie" double CD album, which I'm playing as I write this. Cool!

February 29 – Had another pleasant evening in the Bell yesterday that rounded off the weekend nicely. Matt Brant, not there Friday, got me a birthday pint – thanks!

The only bad aspect was learning that my mate Sam's tooth problem had got so bad she'd been kept in hospital overnight pending possible surgery. Hope she's okay.

More bad news on the comedy front – Frank Kelly, a star of the excellent sitcom *Father Ted*, has died aged 77. He was diagnosed with Parkinson's disease last year.

Father Ted – named in Chapter Two as my sixth favourite UK sitcom ever, centred on the hilarious antics of a mismatched and hopeless trio of Irish priests sharing a house on a remote island.

Kelly was brilliant as the alcoholic, wheelchair-bound, bad-tempered, foul-mouthed, and randy old codger Father Jack, frequently shouting "drink, "feck" and "girls."

He played many other comic and straight screen and stage parts during a six-decade acting career. But he will always be associated with Jack, a role he made his own.

His passing aptly coincided with the 18th anniversary of the death of co-star Dermot Morgan, who played Father Ted.

The other two main stars were Ardal O'Hanlon as dim protégé Father Dougal and Pauline McLynn, housekeeper Mrs Doyle, obsessed with serving tea and sandwiches.

Graham Norton, Richard Wilson and Clare Grogan were among the famous faces also appearing in the outstandingly well written and acted Channel Four show.

March 1 – Sam's still in hospital and due to have surgery on her mouth today. Hope all goes well and she's home with Carl and her family real soon.

It's surprising and sad they've made her wait there this long – but I guess that's what happens when you're unfortunate enough to have to seek medical help at a weekend.

I'm playing Pink Floyd as I write this. And a film shown on BBC Four television over the weekend reminded me just how impressive the Stone Roses were.

I didn't include them in my published run-down of my top 30 groups of all time – some would say a serious oversight. And I must admit they were good – very good!

Music was my first love – and it will be my last, as John Miles so eloquently put it.

And I would add that rock and roll isn't so much a style of music as a state of mind.

March 2 – Happy birthday to my good mate Jen Clough, who used to work behind the bar at the Bell, and Tara Seawright, another friend and former barmaid there.

And a happy third wedding anniversary to my son Phil and his wife Emily. Their big day was one of my own life's highlights and their lovely relationship warms the cockles of this ageing but optimistic cynic's heart.

I've bought a new pair of shoes with my birthday money from my sister Carol and hubby David, and three Dan Brown paperbacks with a W H Smiths token from my "adopted sister" Suzette.

The books are *The Da Vinci Code*, *Inferno* and *Deception Point*. I'm currently reading *The Lost Symbol* and also possess *Digital Fortress* and *Angels and Demons*.

I love Brown's fast-paced thrillers weaving gripping stories round subjects I find fascinating – mysticism, ancient wisdom, hidden histories, powerful secret societies, truth and deception, codes and symbols, spies, assassins and the security services.

March 3 – My beloved sister Jan, Suzette's closest pal, passed away four years ago today. I'll light a candle for her when I get back from the shops.

March 8 – Poor Sam's still suffering with her tooth and jaw infection. Poole Hospital told her surgery was needed but they couldn't do it until her chest can cope – she's an asthmatic. They prescribed strong painkillers until it eases enough to operate safely.

Meanwhile I've had tooth issues of my own. After my six-monthly check up a couple of weeks ago, my dentist said I needed a filling. So I went back yesterday to have it.

I can't imagine anyone enjoying a visit to the dentist – unless they're masochistic or just downright peculiar. But for me it's a right palaver.

I have to take an amoxicillin anti-biotic solution an hour before any dental treatment – even my half-yearly clean. My cardiac consultant and my own doctor both stress the importance of this as any mouth infection getting into my bloodstream could be fatal.

My GP, Dr Tim Mitchell, put it so poetically, saying it would make a bee-line for my heart and the effect could be like a direct hit from a bullet. So you can imagine my nervousness every time I see my dentist, lovely as she is!

With time on my hands before my lunchtime dental appointment and blue skies overhead, I took the opportunity to take a walk to the cliff top yesterday morning to sit for a while taking in the fresh air and sea view. Invigorating!

And talking of life's little pleasures, I've been playing my usual varied mixture of music on my CD player in the past few days – David Bowie, the Stone Roses, Patti Smith and Keane. And I'm listening to UFO as I type. Sweet!

My little financial windfall is disappearing fast so it looks like I'll have to re-apply for benefits, seeing as work in the accepted sense – paid or unpaid – is beyond me these days. Rats! – Oh well, It's been nice to have no money worries for nearly four years.

It really angers me that people look down their noses at those receiving housing, unemployment, sickness or disability benefits. But let's be clear about this.

Aren't those getting tax credits, child allowances and other perks, even though many of them are notably better off, also being subsidised by the State? Of course they are.

And how many relatively (or obscenely wealthy) politicians have quite happily taken money from our benevolent welfare system in the past?

Yet these same odious characters now have the gall to order swingeing cuts in others' lifeline payments using the flimsy, ridiculous excuse they're saving the country cash!

Such nauseating hypocrisy really does stick in my gullet.

March 9 – More bad news for the music world – record producer Sir George Martin, the "fifth Beatle", has died at the age of 90.

He worked with many famous music stars but is best known for his outstanding collaborations with the Fab Four.

In fact, he was the perfect producer for them because he encouraged their wayward genius and shared their open-mindedness and constant drive to do something different and interesting.

He helped compose and arrange their songs and played the keyboard solo on the Rubber Soul album track In My Life.

Classically-trained George had never worked with pop artists before they met – his forte was novelty comedy records with people like the Goons (who the Beatles loved).

They hit it off immediately and John Lennon said they did a lot of learning together in the studio. The results were sensational, transforming music as they ripped up the rule book and kicked down door after door with their trailblazing work.

George was very much a part of the Beatle family, along with manager Brian Epstein, press officer Derek Taylor, road manager Neil Aspinall and his assistant Mal Evans.

In other words, he was in the inner circle of trusted close friends. Indeed, the musicians themselves fully embraced the "fifth Beatle" tag he earned from outsiders.

Coincidentally, over the past few days I've been watching yet again my DVDs of the Beatles Anthology television mini-series, in which George Martin features heavily.

I'll continue watching it later today with an added tinge of sadness. I'll also be playing the group's albums over the next few days.

I actually played a live Paul McCartney CD the other day, featuring many of Paul's biggest hits that Martin originally produced on record. RIP George – and thanks!

Incidentally, I've also been playing a bit of Gary Moore.

March 11 – Wishing a happy birthday to my friend Ryan Bevis, although this one, his 29th, will be tinged with sadness as it will be his first without his mum Theresa, who passed away in January, aged just 50.

I mentioned earlier in this book that dear Theresa was one of the best and closest pals I've ever had. We went through a lot together, good and bad.

One of our many joyful shared experiences was that crazy holiday with mates in Devon in September 1994, referred to in my first book, Chronicles of a Lost Soul.

Ryan was just seven when we went on that excursion but I did comment on writing about it later that often he acted more grown up than the seven adults he was with.

Flippin' 'eck – where did those 22 years go? Frightening, innit?

March 12 – Prog rock pioneer Keith Emerson, 71, has died at his Los Angeles home, apparently from a self-inflicted gunshot wound to the head.

His passing is being treated as suicide but the reason remains shrouded in mystery. Was he terminally ill or just unable to cope with life's rigours? No doubt an inquest will shed some light.

But one thing's for sure – this is a huge shock for the music world due to the keyboardist's stature as one of progressive rock's finest performers.

His musical brilliance was matched by his dazzling skills for showmanship. He used to spin his bulky instruments around, lie on them, lay them on top of himself and stab them with knives to hold the chords down – and all while playing blistering solos.

Yorkshire-born Emerson was in The Nice back in the 1960s before getting together with guitarist Greg Lake and drummer Carl Palmer in 1970 to form one of rock's first "super groups."

The trio – with Lake on lead and bass guitars and vocals – were right up there with Yes and Genesis as undisputed leaders in the prog rock field. I love all three groups.

I had the enormous pleasure of seeing ELP at Bournemouth International Centre in 1992 and they were superb. My mate Lance, one of the local lads drafted in to help shift the band's equipment, later gave me his ELP road crew tee-shirt.

I still have it – it's a treasured memento – but it no longer fits me. I've also had many of the group's albums in my possession over the years.

Switching subjects at some speed, I had a nice trip down Memory Lane yesterday evening as my mate Sam and I recalled good times spent at Boscombe's old Home Guard Social Club and the flat she once had at Christchurch Road, no far from here.

March 14 – I've been selecting more delectable sounds to emanate from my stereo system – the Stranglers, Hazel O'Connor, the

Eagles, Jeff Beck, ZZ Top, Daft Punk, Metallica… and, of course, the Beatles and ELP.

March 16 – Ye gods! – And another piece of my crazy-paved youth has been wrenched from the bizarre jigsaw puzzle I call my life.

Thunderbirds co-creator Sylvia Anderson has passed away aged 88 at her Berkshire home after a short illness.

Sylvia and husband Gerry, who died at Christmas 2012, were jointly behind the top TV puppet adventure programme that millions of us grew up with and loved.

Sylvia voiced Lady Penelope, a character that, like the five crime-busting Tracy brothers and their hi-tech land, sea, air and space rescue vehicles, spawned a merchandising bonanza of Thunderbirds toys, figurines and costumes.

The Andersons also produced other hit children's puppet shows including *Supercar*, *Fireball XL5* and *Stingray*. But *Thunderbirds* was the biggest and most enduring.

It was mainly made at Bray Studios just outside Maidenhead, but occasionally used a factory unit at Slough Trading Estate, just round the corner from the Mars complex making the world-famous chocolate bars and the office block filmed for the opening credits of Ricky Gervais' TV comedy *The Office*.

I used to walk to and from school through the estate and passed all three premises five days a week. One afternoon I saw them filming Thunderbirds through the window of the unit, which was by a railway bridge I crossed as I left the estate on my way home.

Sylvia died at her home in Bray earlier today.

Chancellor of the Exchequer George Osborne is poised to inflict yet another vicious, hurtful budget on us any minute now. As usual he'll be targeting the most needy – disabled, ill, older people, the poor and disadvantaged – supposedly to save money.

Yeah right – What a total git!

Meanwhile his Tory chums are again claiming that the total of jobless people in our country continues to fall. Hey, a flock of pot-bellied porkies has just flown overhead! Actually, porkies is about right – is my assertion any more ridiculous than theirs?

It seems that on one hand they want to scare us silly with dire warnings of disease, economic collapse, foreigners and terrorists but on the other they try to tell us unemployment's down and the country on the up with a bright future thanks to them.

Well, if it is and you're taking us to a new promised land, why more cuts? Why austerity at all? You're making no sense, Tory boys and girls. You're just screwing us over once again. You can't have it both ways you know! – You spiteful tossers!

March 17 – Happy Saint Patrick's Day! It's also a fitting time to honour my good friend Pat Jones, Carole and Tom's mum, who was named Patricia because she was born on this day a few decades back.

Liverpudlian Pat, who's always in my heart but sadly no longer with us physically, was a lovely lady – warm, wise and witty. Incredibly perceptive, she had your number within five minutes of meeting you and could spot a phoney a mile off.

She was kind and generous but formidable if crossed. She could destroy pretensions and delusions of grandeur with a withering dose of skilled sarcasm – still smiling.

Boy, did she have style! She immediately took me under her protective wing and we had some great times and right good laughs together. I miss them and her – a lot.

On discovering we shared a sun sign, Pat started calling me her little Pisces pal – a label that stuck, I'm pleased to say. I've lit a candle for her and put a short tribute on Facebook. It had to be done.

Someone who's just joined Pat in the afterlife is TV conjurer turned compere Paul Daniels, having passed on at the age of 77 after being diagnosed with a brain tumour.

Middlesbrough-born Daniels made his name as a stage magician – of the trick and illusion kind – before moving on to TV, ending up as the host of the quiz shows *Odd One Out*, *Every Second Counts* and *Wipeout*.

His personality grated with me but he was an excellent illusionist – and popular. RIP.

March 18 – Playing Ian Dury and the Blockheads as I type. Have also listened to the excellent Ellie Goulding and more Beatles during the past few days.

But yesterday being St Paddy's Day I went all Irish with the Undertones and the Boomtown Rats. A few hours later I strolled to the Bell, where I had a super session.

My mates Jem Hannen and Mark "Tich" Hemington were there, along with Dawn Lewis and Penny Williams. Penny's daughter, Bell bar manager Nicola, her feller Mark, Matt Brant, Dave and Sam Lowney, Ollie Okoye, John Palmer, Billy Clarkson, Ross Maslin and pub guv'nors Laura Williams and Mark Evans were also present.

And the live music, a fine selection of great rock numbers, was performed with skill, style and humour by pianist Matt Black and his equally talented guitarist pal. It was a very good night in my local watering hole.

For my pub visit I donned my Black Star Riders tee-shirt. This excellent group, which I've seen live twice in the last three years, is the reincarnation of legendary Irish rock band Thin Lizzy, fronted by its former members Scott Gorham (guitars, vocals), Damon Johnson (guitars, vocals) and Ricky Warwick (lead vocals).

Their concert sets feature Lizzy classics alongside their own very Lizzy-sounding material. Their two albums, that I have, are succulent slices of intelligent hard rock.

And talking intelligent rock, I've just finished listening to the late, great Ian Dury and now I'm playing the quite wonderful Disintegration album by the Cure. Sweet!

March 19 – Had a nice few hours yesterday (Friday) round Sam and Carl's with them, their little boys Rudy and Bailey, Sam's adult son Alex, Tina Mcauley, Rich Jeffery, Jem Hannen and the family's two pet dogs Albert and Bramble.

So that made two evenings on the trot spent with friends having drinks and laughs.

I'm having a no-booze quiet night in tonight. I might go to the pub again tomorrow – I'll see how I feel. I like the quieter, mellower Sunday night sessions.

Top story on this morning's news is the resignation of the government's work and pensions secretary Iain Duncan Smith, a former leader of the Conservative Party.

IDS, as he's commonly known, is quoted as saying Chancellor George Osborne's plan to further cut disabled people's benefits is "not defensible" as it coincides with better-off folk get tax reductions.

So it seems even top Tories are sickened and repulsed by wannabe party supremo Osborne and current Prime Minister David Cameron's cruel and insane policies targeting and penalising the nation's most vulnerable people. But hang on a minute.

Cameron's reported as being puzzled by IDS' decision. So am I.

As work and pensions secretary for the past six years, he's been the guy leading the government's scythe attack on the welfare state hitting the poor and disadvantaged.

So it's more than a bit rich for him to suddenly get a conscience and baulk at the continuation of a programme he's been in charge of and quite happy to champion up to now. What a shame he didn't oppose the plans when he was still in the job!

March 20 – More has apparently come to light on the IDS resignation. Fellow Tories are now claiming the real reason he's gone is that he wants us to leave the European Union and will vote for us to do so in the forthcoming referendum.

This puts him in direct opposition to Cameron, Osborne and cabinet chums who want us to stay in with grave warnings of serious consequences if we leave.

I fear that very regrettably they're right – it's too late to leave now. Our leaders should have resisted being sucked into the all-powerful Euro spider's web decades ago when they had several chances to but kept failing to stand up for our country.

And I suspect IDS' critics are wrong – there's no logic in quitting a job as work and pensions overseer because you disagree with your colleagues over Europe.

Why not just say you're leaving the government because you disagree with its leaders' stance in the EU debate? Makes no difference so why not just be honest?

It's all very baffling and whatever IDS or his opponents claim, his real motivation for resigning remains a mystery.

It certainly isn't concern over the clearly cruel and unfair benefit cuts, because if it was he would have acted years ago, not spearheaded them!

IDS reminds me of Liberal Democrat Nick Clegg, another spineless turncoat who actively supported the old coalition government's brutal right-wing policies as Deputy Prime Minister – only to have the gall to criticize them at the last election!

You will notice I've returned to politics after a bit of a hiatus. I've also been watching Adam Curtis films again, plus other thought-provoking documentaries on You Tube. I'm once again feeding my head, stimulating my brain, questioning and seeking truth.

For six months in the recent past I was distracted. My mind was mesmerized, under the enticing spell of a powerful, plausible and ultimately deeply damaging illusion.

It was lovely while it lasted. I had hopes and dreams, I could look to the future with new enthusiasm and confidence and I felt reinvigorated. Then, in an instant, the spell was broken and the fairy tale was brutally revealed as just that, a wicked deception.

Now I'm back, eager to continue my quest to locate the real facts behind the façades, grow in wisdom and spirituality and be a better, more enlightened person.

Please don't misunderstand – it was a beautiful distraction, even though it coaxed me to take my eye off the ball. Other nice diversions include sitting overlooking the sea, immersing myself in terrific music and spending quality time with family and friends.

Part of me craves such experiences. The fairy tale served an energizing purpose in convincing me of certain possibilities I had thought beyond me now. I'm keen to explore them further – and be with loved ones – while not getting too distracted again.

But I'm aiming to avoid banging on too much about the politicians from this point onwards. That's the plan, anyway. But their actions do upset and anger me – often.

Getting back to Adam Curtis, his fascinating, revealing and sometimes worrying productions are right up my street – challenging conventional reality and ideas.

Another film on You Tube, not made by him, is called *The Corporation* – a scathing attack on the power and devastating actions of uncaring companies.

It's a harrowing 2003 Canadian documentary written by University of British Columbia law professor Joel Bakan, directed by Mark Achbar and Jennifer Abbott.

Then there's *Strawman – the Nature of the Cage*, John K Webster's jaw-dropping probe into what the words lawful and legal actually mean.

They're two very separate things apparently – but deliberately treated as the same by police forces and others in authority in their attempts to control and manipulate us.

Lawful refers to the laws of the land, steeped in English history, whereas legal refers to contracts and bureaucracy, starting with your birth certificate and continuing with driving licences, mortgages and all other the bits of paper you sign during your life.

I'd thoroughly recommend both films and anything by Curtis – they're proper eye-openers, I can tell you!

Another one worth checking out is Ross Ashcroft's 2012 film *Four Horsemen*, about the banking and economic systems that create the extremes of wealth and poverty that in turn cause sharp splits, resentment, friction and ultimately war.

Sounds a bit apocalyptic and it certainly is – the real meaning of apocalypse being revelation not Armageddon, as I've just recently learned.

The Bible's Book of Revelations is often interpreted as a symbolism-soaked prophesy of the end times and the total obliteration of our world. Many fear this is imminent.

But, just like Nostradamus' predictions, the account actually has a happy ending – for those left – as all the death and destruction paves the way to a fresh start and renewed hope as a bright dawn heralds the birth of a golden age for mankind.

In addition to viewing these films that are all new to me, I've also been intrigued and alarmed all over again by viewing Curtis' potent mind-benders *Bitter Lake*, the *Power of Nightmares*, the *Living Dead* and *Pandora's Box*.

All these documentaries address vital issues affecting us all that those ruling over us don't want us to know the real facts about.

Seek these productions out on You Tube and open your minds people – even though the stark truth unveiled might well shock you to your roots, as it did me.

Some fascinating thoughts crossed my mind yesterday (Sunday) afternoon while I watched a documentary about secret societies and particularly the Freemasons.

It told how during the Enlightenment period of the seventeenth and eighteenth centuries, the Masonic movement became transformed from an alliance of stone workers into a cultured gentlemen's club, thanks largely to people like philosopher Immanuel Kant and scientist Isaac Newton.

The thoughts that came to me were these:

Science linked to mysticism can spark light and hope, while technology lacking spirituality poses serious threats to us all.

March 22 –Two explosions at an airport and one at a metro (underground) station earlier today killed 13 people and wounded 35 in the Belgian capital of Brussels.

The death toll continues to rise each hour as the TV news programmes cover these traumatic events, thought to be a terrorist attack. Someone is reported to have shouted in Arabic just before one of the blasts.

Okay, that last bit sounds a shade too clichéd, fanciful and convenient for my liking but it is true that the explosions come just four days after the arrest of a guy said to be suspected of involvement in the Paris terror attacks that killed 130 last November.

There are strong suspicions that all these factors point to the guiding hand of the violent and savage extremist network called Islamic State.

But one thing's for sure – there's a chilling echo of the London Bombs of 2005.

Security services in Belgium, France, the UK and other territories are on high alert after these latest atrocities.

So the Third World War rages on. But unless we're among those unfortunate enough to be directly involved – in London, Brussels, Paris or any of those Middle Eastern countries being torn apart by it – millions of us continue with our normal daily lives.

This is because the nature of warfare has changed. No longer are there huge battlefields or miles of trenches full of combatants on competing sides. There are no Hitlers or Napoleons we can identify as the bad guys leading huge compliant armies.

Modern warfare is fought on many fronts – through missiles and the internet, skirmishes, guerrillas, snipers and terrorists and the powerful media of propaganda.

So just when did this Third World War begin? Opinions will vary but events like 911, the London Bombs, the invasions of Afghanistan and Iraq and the recent air strikes in Syria have all been pivotal features raising the stakes for us all.

I would suggest that the roots of the current global ideological battle between radical Islamic doctrine and brutal westernized neo-conservatism stretch all the way back through the other two world wars and far beyond into the mists of antiquity.

The more recent crusades – and leading politicians have knowingly called them that – targeting bloodlust Islamic extremism hark back centuries to the original crusades against Muslims fought by Richard the Lionheart and others in the Holy Land.

It's no longer a case of the USA and us squaring up to Russia with the daunting prospect of nuclear bombs bringing forth mutually assured destruction – not long ago feared to be the most likely scenario for a Third World War.

Of course some countries still have such weapons; including brutal dictatorships we wouldn't trust as far as we could spit, so the threat of a nuclear annihilation remains. But, for now at least, the war isn't being waged in that way.

It's being fought on the streets of European capitals, in Middle Eastern trouble spots and through the World Wide Web.

And this is where the propaganda aspect really comes into its own with uncensored, unrestricted material bombarding the airwaves. Terrorists have computers now.

But then, how do you define a terrorist? I've said several times in my books that one man's terrorist is another's freedom fighter and it all depends where you stand and how you view any struggle of ideas.

I despise with a vengeance the blood drenched actions of unhinged political psychos quoting religion as a reason for mayhem and the murder of civilians going about their daily business – no matter where this happens.

There certainly seem to be plenty such crazies in the ranks of IS and other violent groups. And that sickens me. But American and British soldiers have also been guilty of the grisly, indiscriminate slaughter of innocents in the Middle East and beyond.

So have French, German, Russian, Italian and, yes no doubt aggressive Belgian nut jobs too. Such deplorable behaviour has plagued our planet over the millennia.

I suppose you could argue that we're now reaping the bitter harvest of seeds we've ourselves sown across the globe – that the bloodlust campaign by Islamic extremists is a backlash against our atrocities, or rather, those sanctioned by our leaders.

As I said, murderous madmen can be found on all sides of sharp cultural clashes and lethal confrontations. But so can legions of decent, honest, sincere but misguided folk trying to make sense of insanity and do what they see as the right thing.

These people consider themselves to be warriors for truth, equality and justice. But their mindset is dangerously warped in my view. I seek the same virtues – peacefully.

It's so terribly ironic that far too many political zealots use holy texts as either their justification or their excuse for fighting and killing.

Especially when I'm utterly convinced that all enlightened scriptures – the Bible, Quran, Torah, Upanishads, Bhagavad-Gita, Buddhist, Druid and others – contain the same eternal divine truth, often written in deep symbolism and potent codes.

But they've been taken far too literally and edited and twisted to give confusing and conflicting impressions – and then ruthlessly used to create friction and division.

Why the codes and symbolism you might ask. Why not just state the divine truth clearly so it can be easily understood?

Good question. Some say the bottom line is so very powerful that it can be lethal in the wrong hands, but joyous and life-affirming in the care of the virtuous that are enlightened, skilled and trusted enough to be given access to the hidden wisdom.

That bottom line is thought to be that mankind has a potential for divinity – and the true purpose of life is to strive towards that divinity. I like that.

Certain devout Christians consider this heresy. But Jesus himself is quoted in the New Testament asserting that the kingdom of Heaven is within us and we can achieve all he has and more.

All this stuff reminds me of two old lyrics of mine…

God ain't perched on some high throne
Locked in a mystic cage
He sparkles bright inside us all
He's risen from the grave

Open your minds, open your hearts
Set your spirits free
We need to find Jerusalem
It's inside you and me.

***Excerpt from 'Look Inside'*, Martin Money**
Aug 16 – Sept 6, 1981

And:

The teachings of Islam and Buddha
The sayings of Jesus and Zen
The wisdom of prophets and angels
Are lost on us ignorant men

The thoughts of the world's greatest thinkers
The words shining honest and bright
The jewels of truth and salvation
Are veiled by our limited sight.

***From 'Pearls Before Swine'*, Martin Money**
July 15–17 1986, revised Oct 12, 2012

Religious leaders continue to misquote and misrepresent texts while politicians persist in trying to sell us false histories of glorious but non-existent pasts in their bid to get us to support their seriously dodgy programmes based on all the wrong values.

And talking of wrong values, our whole western economic system is based on a total fallacy. Only three per cent of the world's money is real in a physical sense and the other 97 per cent is just digits on computer screens.

Meanwhile, our beloved countries ceased to exist decades ago and our entire legal set-up revolves around a false perception of our identities. Come again?

Apparently, the United States, Canada, France, the UK and other territories became corporations in the 1930s to avoid bankruptcy as the world economy collapsed.

And we each have a small corporation formed in our name when our parents register our births and receive a certificate to say they've done so.

They thus sell us to the corporation called the United Kingdom and from that point on we're chattels to be traded like commodities.

Our flesh and blood bodies and the consciousness they contain become linked to a legal document then used to identify us. Others follow through our lives – driving licences, mortgage agreements and all paperwork bearing our signatures.

This is precisely why police officers ask you for your name, age and address. Giving them these details means you're voluntarily linking yourself to your paperwork, that is, your corporation. It thus gives the copper authority over you.

Most people don't realize that they're perfectly within their rights under Common Law – the law of the land – to decline to give their particulars, which removes the officer's legal right to detain and interview you. You can walk away – lawfully.

Of course to do so would be foolish, particularly if you've done nothing wrong. It would raise further suspicions and could land you with a whole cartload of hassle.

But that, it seems, is the law – or rather, the big difference between Common Law and the legal system based on maritime law, in other words the rules of the sea that also cover finance, trading, commerce, wealth and resources, documents and bureaucracy.

Similar situations apply in the United States (that huge corporation, seemingly a totally different entity to the land called America) and other places abroad.

The world's economies and financial systems are run by bankers and totally rely on debt. We constantly relieve each other of money – so at any one time some folk are bound to be missing out. Poverty, homelessness, hunger, disease and death are rife.

The whole rancid pile of garbage and crap stinks to high heaven. It's a disgrace.

I've learned all this from watching You Tube documentaries. I wasn't aware of the scale of the deceptions before, although I did know some of the facts.

Critics will no doubt claim these aren't facts at all but wild allegations cooked up by fruit loop conspiracy theorists and deluded fantasists.

But I'm pretty sure this is a far more accurate summary of the truth than the false claims of those wanting to control us at every turn. Slaves to the system? – absolutely!

Am I right or have I been seriously misled? I guess it all boils down to what you feel in your gut, your intuitive instincts guided by your higher self.

Granted we're not bound in chains, whipped and forced to perform heavy labour as happened in the past. But it's a sobering thought that the relative wealth we've enjoyed in the west for yonks was amassed breaking the backs of those poor souls.

March 23 – Had a nice afternoon with Paula yesterday at the Bell. It was my monthly rendezvous with my very good, long-standing friend for a few bevvies and a catch up.

March 24 – Dream-weaver politicians spin glittering yarns about a fictitious past. It's all far too clearly-defined, infantile and simplistic, too right and wrong, good and evil, us and them, totally ignoring the complexities of human behaviour and interactions.

Their talk of glorious bygone days they want to restore takes no account of the subtleties, weaknesses, mistakes and diplomacy that typify existence. Or the selfish, cowardly, callous and greedy impulses guiding people's actions for that matter.

The Brussels death toll has reached 31, including two brothers said to have been suicide bombers. It's now estimated that 300 were injured, many critically.

Islamic State is said to have claimed responsibility for the attacks.

A manhunt has been launched for a third suspect – also thought to have been involved in the Paris attacks – as a traumatized Belgian nation tries to come to terms with it all.

Another item on today's TV news focussed on the trial of 70-year-old Radovan Karadzic, who faces multiple charges of genocide and crimes against humanity during the Bosnian War in the 1990s during which 100,000 died.

This bloody stain on European history was another phase of the ideological conflict that's rumbled on for centuries. Muslims suffered greatly in that particular part of it. Another reason for the rise of the radical, violent Islamic backlash? I'd say so.

And it's just been announced on the news that football legend Johann Cruyff has passed away aged 68. The former smoker was told he had lung cancer last October.

His dazzling skills typified the Netherlands national side's attractive and highly effective style called total football.

Cruyff won three consecutive European Cups with Ajax as a player and went on to manage Barcelona to their first European Cup win in 1992.

In summary, the world of football has lost one of its all-time greatest exponents.

March 25 – Radovan Karadzic has been sentenced to 40 years' imprisonment. So, now aged 70, he's likely to die in jail.

So another monster's behind bars. We can breathe a sigh of relief and sleep easier in our beds. The world's safer again. Do you really believe that? – Nah, me neither.

It's Good Friday today, a sacred time for Christians, the day their Lord was killed. Sunday will be celebration time, the day he is said to have been raised from the dead.

Really? So why do the dates vary from year to year? Because they're governed by the phases of the moon, that's why. But Jesus was said to represent the supreme sun God.

Okay, I'm not going to go over old ground about the religion's many overlaps with pre-Christian customs and festivals and the striking similarities between its stories and those of other, older belief systems. But I will mention a couple of interesting facts.

One is that in the heart of Vatican City, global centre of the Roman Catholic Church, stands a pagan fertility symbol in the form of an obelisk brought over from Egypt.

There's another in Washington DC and a third beside the Thames in London – Cleopatra's Needle.

In fact, these four-sided towering spike-like structures topped with pyramids can also be found in France, Argentina and around the world. Why is this do you think?

I'd suggest the reason is that that all humanity's major faiths have the same root source, dating from the old pagan religion of ancient Egypt with its many gods and one supreme deity, Ra, symbolized by the sun (and even further back than that!).

This is why so many of the stories told in the sacred texts of diverse faiths throughout history are so very similar. They're the same story told over and over again.

So all religions try to grasp and convey the same basic truths, making it bitterly ironic that they're so often pitched against each other in blood soaked conflicts.

Many people believe that the sun as we know it is a recurring theme because it's so aptly symbolic, providing us with warmth, light and sustenance.

But I heard recently that some say in fact all the solar references in ancient texts and artwork actually refer to Saturn, the planet linked to dark practices and Satanism.

This is possible, of course, but I prefer to think it means our positive life-giving sun. It's the optimist in me, you see.

Incidentally, the Vatican, Washington and the City of London are the three great power houses of the modern world, just like Egypt was in its day.

All three are independent sovereign states, completely separate from the cities and countries they're in. They're a law unto themselves and they jointly rule over us all.

In fact, the City of London – the Crown – is the most wealthy and influential square mile on the face of the planet.

And, although that great superpower the United States is said to have shaken free from British control in the 18th century, in truth it is still governed by the Crown, financially and politically. So is Canada, Australia and places across the globe.

And when I say the Crown, I mean it in the real sense – the City of London. Not the Queen or the Monarchy, that's a common misconception, conveniently for some.

And the Crown is – a corporation. Just like the United States, Microsoft, the United Kingdom, Exxon, Canada, Wal-Mart, France, General Electric, Ford, countless much smaller firms, you, me and everyone with a birth certificate.

Or rather, the paperwork-based entities created in our names when our births are registered, as opposed to the flesh, bone, organ and blood bodies containing our sparks of consciousness – the real us.

If John and Mary Smith decide to form a company, they gather together all the paperwork to assemble a separate entity – just as much a person under the terms of our legal system as the couple who created it.

This also happens when two friends follow the same process, or indeed, just one individual. If you create a company – a corporation – in your name, it becomes a different being from you.

It can be sued or go bankrupt just as you can. But if either happens to it, that doesn't apply to you, and vice-versa.

It's called limited liability – which is why many UK firms' names end in Ltd (Corps in the USA).

And it's also the reason we're constantly asked to sign bits of paper. It links us to the separate entity bearing our name that the whole legal and financial system relies on to function.

The whole world is run on money, property and possessions, banking, loans and debt. And most of our reality, built up around such nebulous concepts, is a financial and bureaucratic fallacy. Fact!

****

CHAPTER THREE – PARALLELS AND SIMILARITIES

March 26 – I'm worried about my mate Sam Excell at the moment. She collapsed at her house on Tuesday (22nd) and is in Poole Hospital (again) for tests, scans and observation as staff try to ascertain what caused it. She has several health issues.

I visited her on Thursday (24th) and she didn't look good. She was in a lot of pain, poor girl. I hope they sort her out and send her home real soon.

Yesterday evening (Good Friday) I watched a documentary on BBC Four TV about the late, great Janis Joplin, one of my favourite rock singers of all time.

Born in Texas in January 1943, she moved to California in her early adulthood to make a name as a jazz and blues singer, coming to prominence with the legendary Big Brother and the Holding Company before going solo with her own backing band.

A heavy drinker who also took other drugs including heroin, she died in Los Angeles in October 1970 when she was just 27.

She was friendly, amiable and laughed a lot but interviews with family and friends and readings from her letters home helped give us an insight into the private torture of an extrovert, forceful and animated performer.

Janis came across as a sensitive, troubled and actually quite solitary and sad person despite her many friends and acquaintances and millions of fans across the world.

She liked the company of men and had her lovers, but is quoted as once saying: "On stage I make love to twenty-five thousand people; and then I go home alone."

She's become known as one of the tragic 27 Club of outstandingly skilled rock stars dying at that age. Other members include Jimi Hendrix, Kurt Cobain, Jim Morrison, Amy Winehouse and Rolling Stones founder Brian Jones.

But, like all of them, her music will live forever thanks to her outstanding ability and electrifying shows. What a voice. What a talent. What a shame.

Still on the subject of superb sounds, I'm currently playing a CD of my favourite Rolling Stones album Sticky Fingers, and in the past two days I've also listened to Wishbone Ash, Fleetwood Mac, AC/DC, King Crimson, Girlschool and Supertramp.

And, staying with documentaries while also bringing books into the equation, I find it intriguing that, in my ongoing search for truth I'm finding that the same themes and stories keep cropping up time and time again.

The same words, numbers, imagery, measurements, colours, shapes, symbols, zodiac signs, dates, customs, pictures, creatures and people can be found across the globe throughout recorded history.

I'm sure many of these parallels and similarities point to the potentially unifying force of ancient wisdom lost over the millennia. The evidence is quite compelling.

But I do feel that some obsessive conspiracy theorists take it too far, seeing connections all over the place, wherever they look in fact – even though some of them are pretty tenuous and don't really stand up to close scrutiny.

I think there are probably as many accidental, unconscious correlations as intended ones. Some of the apparent link-ups are just, well, coincidences.

That said, it doesn't stop me being enthralled by all this stuff and thirsty for more.

Turning briefly to the news, our Tory government wants to turn all our schools into academies. What the heck does that mean? What's in a name?

Well, the Oxford English Dictionary definition of academy is a place of study or training in a special field. Makes you wonder what the politicians are on about.

I'd argue that all children must be provided with a firm educational foundation, certainly concentrating on English and mathematics but more generally covering history, geography, economics, the sciences, the arts (including music) and religions.

Handy tips should be given to help them develop vital life skills such as healthy cooking, morals and ethics, money management, exercise, empathy and tolerance.

They shouldn't be even contemplating specializing until they've learned these basics and are approaching adulthood, preparing themselves for different career paths.

But I don't think the Tories are actually talking in terms of the dictionary definition. I'm guessing their idea involves the government directly funding schools itself, wrenching them from local council control.

I always thought Labour was supposed to be the party of more state intervention while the Conservatives wanted less. How things have changed!

I'd be interested to hear what teachers think of Cameron and crew's plan. Would it make any difference to education standards and if so, would they improve or fall?

Why not just carry on calling them schools? Academy sounds far too pretentious.

I'd facetiously suggest that if a name change is required (it's not, by the way), it should better reflect what these places really are – brainwashing plants, system fodder stations, lie factories, indoctrination centres or something like that.

March 27 – Happy birthday former workmate June Wade. And happy Easter all. Yes, it's that Sunday when some go to church and many scoff chocolate eggs.

It's also a great excuse (not that I need one) to once again listen to Patti Smith's classic album Easter – on my CD player now. It's rock and roll at its most potent, mesmerizing and body moving. I saw Patti at Reading Festival in 1978 – brilliant!

I've also played some Talking Heads and Janis Joplin since I wrote my last journal entry. It seems I've gone a bit American. But then, that's where all the music that inspired England's greatest bands and solo stars came from.

Side-stepping rock for a moment, it was good to see our nation's football team beat world champions Germany 3-2 yesterday evening – and in Berlin too!

Sceptics will say it was only a friendly so doesn't count. Try telling the Germans that.

England's exciting young lions were 2-0 down with an hour played but then staged a gripping comeback climaxing with a 90th-minute header by Tottenham's Eric Dier.

Harry Kane, also of Spurs, and Leicester's Jamie Vardy scored the other two goals but 19-year-old Dele Alli, another Tottenham player, was the brilliant star of the show.

No wonder these two clubs are currently first and second in the Premier League table.

This result bodes well for Roy's boys as they prepare for the Euros in France this summer. They play Holland at Wembley in another warm-up friendly on Tuesday.

Something else I watched through my TV set last night was a terrific documentary on You Tube called *Kymatica*. I'd thoroughly recommend it as it puts so eloquently many of the things I've been trying to say in my own clumsy cockeyed way.

For a bit of light relief, I also found Whole Lotta Helter-Skelter on You Tube, and played that. It's an excellent mash up of a pair of great tracks from my two favourite groups, Led Zeppelin and the Beatles. Not everyone likes it, but I think it's great.

March 28 – Happy birthday Paula. Have a wonderful day my friend.

It's Easter Monday and a nice sunny spring morning so I've just been for a wander through Fisherman's Walk to sit for a short while overlooking the bay.

I say short while because there was a strong and chilly breeze blowing, the tail end of last night's violent storm, so it was too cold to hang about too long.

But it was still good to get some fresh air and exercise in such pretty surroundings. I do love Southbourne!

Went to the Bell yesterday evening but it was a tad disappointing – lots of people there but not many I knew except my pals John Gaynor, Jem Hannen and Matt Brant.

Laura and Mark (guv'nors) were also in attendance and my good friend Bev Jones popped in with another old pub regular Tim Robbins but they didn't stay long.

The same went for Pete Rowsen, another former Bell stalwart who was also on that mad and legendary Devon holiday in the nineties, mentioned in my earlier books.

But that was about it. I'll try again tonight to see if more familiar faces are there.

You really get the feeling winter's gone and springtime's here, what with the milder weather, the equinox occurring last week and the clocks going forward yesterday.

Recent heartbreak is slowly healing and I'm able to look forward again, hoping the change in season brings liberal doses of love and happiness, humour and miracles.

More excellent American sounds have been emanating from my stereo system courtesy of Television, Guns'n'Roses and Bob Seger. Plus some tip-top home-grown stuff in the form of Jethro Tull, Clean Bandit, Hawklords, Led Zeppelin and T Rex.

Playing superb albums like Pilgrimage (Wishbone Ash), Marquee Moon (Television), Electric Warrior (T Rex) and Aqualung (Jethro Tull) allows me to revel in the pure glory of rock music. It's one of my great passions, as you've no doubt gathered.

March 29 – Well, I went to the pub yesterday evening and, although generally a lot quieter than Sunday, the small band of drinkers included several people I knew.

Landlord Mark Evans, John Gaynor and Matt Brant were there again, this time joined by Ben Avill, Jenny Daniels and a guy called Ian (don't know his surname but we've been friends for ages and his nickname's Long Shanks because he's tall).

Plus Aussie Stu, a regular called Brian and a feller I've seen there quite a bit in the recent past but last night was the first time we spoke. His name's Darren.

For the second day running I was served by a pleasant young barmaid called Demi – I hope I got the spelling right. She had a different colleague this time, but on both occasions her co-workers were other nice young ladies.

It's always good when your bar staff are pretty, amiable females. Hey, I'm no sexist but I am a red-blooded guy!

Turning to more serious matters, and getting back to what I was saying about the Bosnian War being part of an ongoing ideological struggle stretching back centuries, I'd actually go even further.

Conflicts in the world's trouble spots such as the Ukraine, the Balkans, the Middle East and other places are linked in with terrorist attacks all over and the migrant crisis.

All are part of a ruthless elite's master plan using divide and rule to devastating effect while amassing all the wealth and resources for themselves and bringing in a single world government, religion, currency and army to serve them as they enforce total control over us all.

Events and issues are portrayed as isolated from each other so we don't realize what's really happening. As I said, the Third World War is upon us. And it's getting worse.

Am I sounding like David Icke? Well, I happen to think he's right in much of what he claims. Note I say much, not all. The shape-shifting reptiles bit is especially hard to accept it's so bizarre – but I feel in my gut he's bang on with a lot of his assertions.

And it's not just him saying such things. A growing number of people are coming to much the same conclusions. What they're claiming starts to make sense of the multi-faceted madness we see all around us.

So-called conspiracy theorists are often ridiculed. Yeah, sure, some are obsessed crackpots with crazy ideas – but not all of them.

Maybe one reason many folk react so violently against such people is that to admit there's even a small chance they're right would be far too bleeding scary.

It's a heck of a lot more comfortable and reassuring just to plant your head firmly in the sand and ignore the seemingly wild assertions.

You know the ones – global warming is a myth; the evil cabal in charge wants to kill off billions and thereby reduce the world's population, they're messing with our minds and bodies to make us compliant… and so on.

You what? Well, yes, some citizens are even claiming that our overlords are ensuring that we eat genetically modified foods, ordering the addition of certain toxins to our medications and getting aircraft to spray us with chemical vapour trails to this end.

And other poisons and information gathering or mind-altering microchips can be injected into us without our knowledge using hypodermic needles.

Fluoride, found in many foodstuffs and drinks is apparently good for teeth and added to some water supplies and most toothpaste. It's said to make us more docile and malleable and cause cancer, infertility and brain and bone damage.

Certain other internet whistle-blowers even go along with David Icke's assertion that we're being ruled by cold-blooded alien lizard leaders with different DNA to the rest of us. Sounds ridiculous and completely outlandish but does that make it untrue?

(I can hear some say "yes you dozy pillock, sort yourself out!" – but, unlike others I don't feel in any position to decisively and arrogantly make declarations one way or the other).

Looking at all the insanity and cruelty plaguing our reality certainly makes me wonder. Yes, it all sounds a tad too weird even for me – but I insist on keeping an open mind, the only way to truth. Closed ones are so much easier to fool and control.

March 30 – Oh dear! The Netherlands beat England 2-1 in their friendly football match at Wembley. Vardy scored again for us but our lads were generally lacklustre.

No team likes to lose, even a friendly where there's nothing at stake, but maybe this result isn't so bad. The last thing we wanted was for Roy's boys to go into the Euros over-confident and too complacent after Saturday's thrilling victory over Germany.

It's good to be alert, sharp and aware you're beatable if you slip up. That's how tournaments are won.

March 31 – I'm listening to some really cool tracks laid down by the magnificent Aretha Franklin. Just so you know.

Anyway, a few paragraphs back I referred to people refusing to even contemplate certain possible scenarios because they're too damned frightening. Well, cop this little lot of mind-blowing allegations.

Watching more alternative media presentations on You Tube last night, I gazed open-mouthed at film footage of what were said to be prisons, concentration camps and thousands of temporary coffins all ready for a catastrophe in the United States.

This could be a nuclear strike, economic crash, epidemic or a food and water shortage sparking civil panic and unrest requiring the savage implementation of martial law.

Only in America, the cynics would say – And yes, again, this sounds incredible and totally implausible. Crazy, in fact. It could never happen. Not in the USA, certainly not here. Really? I'm not so sure. Glad you are.

But some of these controversial documentaries, one or two banned from mainstream media, do seem to be put together by people with their own agendas, hidden or not.

There was one, for example, compiled by a fire and brimstone Christian nut claiming that US president Barack Obama and Russia's leader Vladimir Putin were about to plunge us into the final cataclysmic war forecast in the Bible's Book of Revelations.

What really set my alarm bells ringing was the fact that, after trying to terrify viewers for well over two hours, this guy ended up offering to sell them so-called survival kits containing handy tips on how to protect, feed and clothe their families in a crisis.

Two thoughts occurred to me simultaneously. The first was the obvious implication: sod everyone else's families then. That's not very Christian, is it?

The other was: yeah right, okay mate. Couldn't you find something else to flog without scaring people witless? Talk about aggressive marketing!

But, while common themes recur time and time again about ruthless and all powerful leaders manipulating our reality and ushering in a New World Order in which the rest of us are either slaves, prisoners or corpses, it's not all doom and gloom. Honest!

David Icke is one of those who says there is hope and real cause to be optimistic because more and more people across the world are waking up and realizing what the game plan is, therefore gaining the knowledge and power to stop it happening.

When all's said and done, Icke's bottom line is this – infinite love is the only truth; everything else is illusion. I think that's beautiful.

Oh, and I'm now enjoying a CD of Otis Redding songs. I seem have a bit of a soul thing going on at present. A nice counterbalance to all the talk of catastrophes!

Good grief – another comedy legend and childhood hero of mine has kicked the bucket. Ronnie Corbett, half of the Two Ronnies, was 85. The other one, Ronnie Barker, died in 2005.

Both men had successful solo careers and worked with others but they will always be best known for their brilliant double act that at its best rivalled that of Morcambe and Wise. And that's praise indeed! Farewell Ronnie and thanks for all the laughs.

April 1 – There was a worrying item on this morning's TV news about government plans to put more armed police on our streets. They say it's due to the heightened risk of terrorist attacks in the UK following the recent ones in Paris and Brussels.

Bearing in mind the date, who the bleeding hell are they trying to kid?

If there's a greater chance of nut jobs wreaking murderous mayhem here, I'd suggest it's thanks to our politicians' intolerant and aggressive policies at home and abroad.

nd I fear the increase in armed rapid response teams with lethal firearms is all part of the governing elite's unfolding grand scheme to rule over every aspect of our lives by force, with imprisonment and shoot to kill policies if we step too far out of line.

It's another aspect of the relentless march to a global iron fist state where the top dogs have all the power and we have none, all our civil rights having been removed.

The – dare I say – rather convenient terrorist attacks abroad have just given them the perfect excuse, one that far too many citizens wilfully buy into without question.

Crazy, paranoid conspiracy theory? Take another look around.

People used to mock and ridicule David Icke. Some still do. But the one-time largely rejected and isolated author and public speaker now draws audiences of thousands. The tide is turning. More individuals are waking up, just as I did a few years ago.

As I said, I don't necessarily agree with all he claims, especially the more bizarre bits. But I'm not alone in thinking he's on the level and on the button more times than not.

America, Canada, Australia, Europe – his books are being read and his theatre talks selling out all over the world. But he would be the first to urge folk to do their own research and not just take on board what he says without further investigation.

I happen to agree with him that blind acceptance of another's views and assertions without scrutiny or comparison is a major reason we're in such a mess today.

Politicians, preachers, professors and others have all been meekly followed and obeyed as citizens have eagerly given up their freedoms of thought and expression.

It hasn't occurred to them that such apparent authority figures might have their own agendas, and that those agendas might not be all that altruistic.

Icke's critics have called him a Nazi Jew-hater – a wildly inaccurate and ludicrous slur that falls down as soon as anyone can be bothered to hear him or read his books.

I saw one scathing You Tube presentation that drew parallels between David's beliefs and those of Adolf Hitler. The documentary maker was arguing that rather than opposing the New World Order, Icke was actually serving it, knowingly or not.

My response is that knowledge and wisdom can be enlightening and healing or dark and destructive depending on the characters and motives of those with access to them.

Icke shares Hitler's beliefs in the Atlantis legend and the idea that humans can enhance their own divine natures with the right mental tools and use of energies.

But Hitler, motivated by his own inner dark current, twisted that belief to create the master race mentality that led to so much prejudice, savagery, misery and death.

Both men have shown a great interest in occult (hidden) wisdom but again the reasons, interpretations and resultant actions couldn't be more different.

My own readers will know that for years I've advocated the concept of positive and negative energy currents residing within us all, constantly battling for supremacy. Religions have externalised these impulses and labelled them God and Satan.

The creation story, Adam and Eve, Noah and the flood, Cain and Abel, Moses, Abraham, David and Goliath and all those old fables have their roots in truth about the human mind and human nature that jointly aspire to realize our inner divinity.

But the tales have been taken too literally and twisted beyond recognition, obscuring or in some cases even reversing the original messages – causing strife and wars.

So, using the dreadfully misleading and over-simplistic symbolism of the world's three great faiths, we can all be saints and sinners, angels and devils. And we are, all of the time. I can be both in the same day.

But we have to be very careful when speaking of mankind's inner divinity.

I've said in previous books that I feel we are at a crucial point in our evolution, poised to take another huge step towards being a more enlightened and spiritual species.

We're rediscovering our latent skills in several spheres – and especially the awesome power of the human mind, including its ability to influence objects and energies.

Hitler thought this meant we could aspire to be gods and he corrupted the truth to fit his own jet black, sinister and deeply negative worldview of an elite master race.

We all see where that led – mass extermination of millions of poor souls considered inferior stock holding back the progress to that godlike status.

When I mention our inner divinity I'm referring to our higher selves – the lighter, more positive energy currents within us as opposed to our darker, negative ones. These competing impulses make up our individual sparks of consciousness.

And they in turn have become artificially and disastrously separated over the millennia from the One Great Consciousness some call God.

I've often described us as small drops from a massive ocean that will ultimately return there but in the meantime need to combat our false feelings of isolation from the One and each other and realize our true source and destiny.

We are the ocean and it is us. We're indivisible but we've forgotten that we are.

In the beginning was the Word – and the Word was the outward expression of the Thought, in other words, Supreme Consciousness, the force behind everything.

As seekers of truth and light try to find a way through the haze of a complex, confused and seriously compromised reality, agents of the dark side wage wars inflicting much misery and death across the globe.

Radical Islamists resort to sickening barbarism, torturing and beheading innocent people. This is evil and intolerable.

But so are the war crimes committed by Western service personnel in Iraq and Afghanistan, where citizens have been indiscriminately bombed and butchered.

But these are only the modern-day equivalent of the atrocities of Hitler, who killed six million Jews in the 1940s, and the Roman Catholic Church that put 50 million so-called heretics to death in the Middle Ages.

The Iron Maiden and the Wheel were among the grisly devices used by the Inquisition to breaks the bones, tear the flesh and spill the blood of innocent people. And all in the name of the God of Love.

Some say that rather than being a force for good, the Roman Catholic Church is an evil organisation with pagan roots in ancient Babylon and Egypt. Certainly a lot of the customs, artwork, and symbolism seem the same.

Others say it's the Jesuits in particular that are history's bad guys, responsible for the two world wars and the conflicts in Vietnam, Serbia, Iraq and Afghanistan.

The fact that the current Pope is the first Jesuit to ever hold the title is seen as very bad news indeed in some quarters.

But whoever gets blamed – them, the Illuminati, Freemasons, churches, political organisations or other groupings – you can bet the ones pointing the finger will have their own agendas. Listen to all sides and keep that mind wide open. They hate that!

Besides, things are rarely that clear-cut. There are bad apples in all baskets.

Is David Icke a false prophet? Possibly, but if he is, he's a lot more frigging convincing than the politicians, priests and power freaks whose bold assertions seem at best confused and far too frequently just plain contradictory.

A bit earlier I was talking about ancient wisdom, the energies that motivate us and the power of the human mind. Which brings me on to noetic science.

I was blissfully unaware of this fascinating field of research until I read Dan Brown's book the *Lost Symbol*. I've just finished it and I'm now on his more famous best-seller the *Da Vinci Code*.

Noetic science explores with lab tests and other means the effects consciousness can have on the physical world. This is a fact. Literally, the exercise of mind over matter.

There's nothing new in the theory – the ancient Greek philosophers Plato and Aristotle both expounded its possibilities. But it's only now that science is properly investigating what they and others have been saying for millennia.

Like quantum physics, this is another example of how cutting edge technology is now confirming what mystics and other wise thinkers of old knew all along.

It's a very encouraging feature of the reunion of hard factual science and the more fluid realms of philosophy and spirituality – disciplines that were torn apart ages ago and for far too long considered to be at odds with each other, competing for validity.

Keeping with the union theme, you might have been wondering why a guy like me who's so hot on love and peace, harmony and togetherness is so opposed to the idea of a single world government.

In principle I'm not, any more than I'm against the principle of a European Union or our own United Kingdom. In my heart I'm with all three. Of course I am.

But it all gets a bit fragmented and messy when politics rears its ugly head. It's the motives behind such power blocks that worry me. And the forms they take.

When it comes to the UK, I fervently support full co-operation between England, Scotland and Wales – with the vital proviso that they each retain their own distinct identities, sovereignty and independence.

Northern Irish people, like those of the Falklands and other British territories, should have the final say over whether they stay with us or strike out on their own forming other alliances, with majority votes deciding the issue in a truly democratic manner.

I feel exactly the same about the EU but my concern over the way it's so quickly turned from a mutually beneficial trading agreement into a huge monolithic law-enforcing bureaucratic Frankenstein monster is well documented.

Worried as I am, I fear it's far too late to back out, which could be disastrous for our economy. Our best option now is to stay in and hope that our leaders stand up for our interests instead of rolling over and giving away our power as they have in the past.

But it's not too late to halt the acceleration towards a global government, currency, army and religion in a sinister liberty-crushing New World Order.

It's interesting to note that some, like me, are deeply concerned that this could be a fascist state, a larger version of Hitler's German empire. Some Americans worry it could be an equally vicious communist regime like Stalin's USSR.

These sound like much the same thing to me – Dictatorial iron fist set ups denying basic human rights and treating us like slaves, pawns in their twisted games.

And these lethal games would ensure that all the wealth and power stayed firmly at the top of society's pyramid.

Cynics would say this is exactly what we have already, masked by the pretence of a democratic system that's being dismantled by the day. I fear they're right.

I've even seen claims that violent Islamic extremism is a front for the brutal New World Order agenda. But this could just be a ploy to demonize Muslims.

And when it comes to religions, I say follow the one you wish by all means – or none – but accept and respect others' rights to the same freedom of choice and under no circumstances harass them or use faiths as excuses for political division and wars.

One thing I am sure of is that servants of the vicious, unscrupulous elite running our reality are infiltrating all sections of society – whether they're based on culture, ideology, religion, nation or political views – stirring them up to oppose each other.

So if you're a passionate anything – Tory, socialist, Green, Muslim, Christian, Jew, Englishman, American or Turk – you can be putty in the hands of a manipulator who has no allegiance to anyone or anything except the wicked agenda he shares with other members of the ruling cabal.

April 2 – Barack Obama was on the TV news today warning of the growing threats of terrorism and nuclear attack. He mentioned Islamic State by name.

He's also recently identified North Korea and Russia as nations to watch closely. Here we go. Fasten your seat belts girls and boys.

Yes, it worries us all that aggressive states either possess nuclear weapons or might obtain them. But to date the United States is the only country ever to have dropped a nuclear bomb on another – Japan, twice within a week.

It's a bit rich for nations with their own nuclear devices to vehemently oppose others having the same type of weaponry. It takes hypocrisy to a whole new level.

We can't un-invent nuclear weapons, so the only real, logical answer is a total ban on all such bombs and missiles. But who would enforce it? – A world-governing body. See the problem?

As I said, I've no issue with the concept of unifying global forces, but I have huge reservations over and a spine-chilling fear of who would actually be in charge.

I also oppose the centralisation of too much power in the hands of too few people – advocating a move in the opposite direction, back to more grass-roots democracy.

And even if there were no nuclear threats, chemical or biological warfare could have similarly disastrous consequences for humanity.

I suppose you could argue that the United Nations, set up after World War Two, is a peace-keeping world army of sorts.

Maybe retaining national banks, armies, governments and currencies is the solution but having universal forums to work together in a bid to tackle shared problems and maintain peace and equality – just as we're theoretically supposed to have now.

Many claim that at the core of the ruling elite are 13 bloodlines that have held on to power throughout human history.

So descendants of the Pharaohs have ruled Europe and the UK for hundreds of years and some have been presidents of the United States.

It's certainly true that the Bush family and others have proudly flaunted their ancestral links to our current Royal family and other crowned heads stretching back centuries.

Some people also claim that these bloodlines are very nasty people indeed.

David Icke famously goes further, saying they have a different DNA to the rest of us, an alien-human hybrid. That's why they interbreed with each other – to preserve the blood's purity. The Egyptians apparently indulged in incest for the same reason.

Which brings us on to other taboo sexual topics – rape and paedophilia. Again, Icke and others allege that both are commonplace among the ruling elite. Their altered DNA means they can't feel the same emotions or revulsion that we do.

This, suggests Icke, is precisely why the now-disgraced deejay, TV presenter and charity fundraiser Jimmy Savile could carry on his sick and perverted practices for decades and they didn't become public knowledge until after he died.

He was well in with some very powerful people, procured victims for their equally twisted activities and was therefore shielded and protected by them, claims Icke.

Daft as a brush Dave goes further still, saying the elite are Satanists who perform human sacrifices and have a taste for necrophilia.

If this seems outrageously beyond the pale, please bear in mind that certain assertions have recently come to light that Savile sexually abused mental patients and corpses as well as scores of little children. Which would make him one very sick predator.

But I do stress that these aren't my claims but others' – against a dead bloke.

And it's alleged that these dark and dangerous individuals, unelected and hiding in the shadows, run everything – governments, monarchies, banks and business, religions, the media, entertainment, councils, public services, pharmaceuticals, everything.

Icke and many others cite the Illuminati, but this is denied by an anonymous internet contributor who says he's a high-ranking member and they're actually the good guys fighting the dark elite in charge. As always, I'm keeping an open mind.

It's further said that pop stars including Lady Gaga, Katy Perry, David Bowie and the Beatles have used Illuminati references, symbolism and hand gestures.

Blimey! Its Orwell's 1984 meets Huxley's *Brave New World* and the Matrix movies.

But alien shape-shifting lizards? Sounds incredible, but in light of all the above…

Phew! – After that, I think it's time to return to the mundane world of conventional reality.

Sam came out of hospital Thursday so I'm popping in to see her this evening on my way to the Bell to meet friends and watch local tribute band Total Madness.

On the CD front, I've been listening to the Fall, Dire Straits and the Damned.

April 3 – Yesterday was very enjoyable. As planned, I went to Sam's for a few drinks before trundling off to the pub for even more bevvies in the company of mates and local tribute band Total Madness, who I hadn't seen before. They were good.

Lots of friends were there, but I'll just mention Rod Marlow, John Gaynor, Matt Brant, John Palmer, Chris Davis and Jem Hannen.

I had my weekly alcohol quota in one day. Oops! – Not good and won't be doing it again in a hurry. Shh – please don't tell my doctor!

I'm currently listening to Time Flies, the excellent Oasis compilation album. That Noel Gallagher feller really is a superbly skilled songwriter – great rock and roll tunes linked to intelligent, poetic lyrics with that surreal twist I love.

His Beatle references (wonder wall, yellow submarine and so on) and musical style make clear one of his major inspirations. His brother Liam, the Oasis lead vocalist, has also publicly acknowledged the Fab Four's influence on them.

April 5 – Reading the *Da Vinci Code* is an interesting pastime having seen the movie starring Tom Hanks that was based on the novel.

As always, books can go into more detail about certain aspects of stories than adrenalin-pumping thriller films.

In the case of the *Da Vinci Code*, this includes the emphasis on the sacred feminine principle important to ancient religions but largely rejected by Christianity with its massive reliance on all things male – apostles, priests and so on.

The Roman Catholic Church in particular has demonized the blissful, wonderful and potentially divine act of sexual union, portraying it as something dirty and sinful.

But paradoxically, the Church has recognized and honoured the sacred feminine by elevating Jesus' mother Mary to a status rivalling his – albeit as an unsullied virgin.

Consequently, perceptions have become warped as perfectly natural and normal impulses have been repressed. They've broken out, as they would do, with messed up minds instigating society's more hated activities such as paedophilia and bestiality.

This is a wholly unsatisfactory state of affairs and I strongly advocate restoring the balance between male and female principles. After all, the energy, the consciousness we call God, is a perfect blend of both, above and beyond narrow gender definitions.

Jesus only referred to God the Father because he was addressing a strictly patriarchal society. But he had females in his inner circle – a fact acknowledged by Christianity.

I'd suggest that Mary Magdalene and the sisters Martha and Mary were as important to Him as Simon Peter or the other male apostles, a fact glossed over by the Church.

Actually it's a weird old faith, Christianity. It's supposed to be a monotheistic religion centred on the One True God, but Roman

Catholicism has absorbed many pagan faith features such as the pantheon of lesser Roman/Greek deities, calling them saints.

And talking of gods, have you noticed that Islamic State is a shorter version of ISIS (standing for the Islamic State of Iraq and Syria) – which is also the name of an Egyptian goddess?

Isis was the wife of the great god Osiris and mother of Horus. She's often cited as an earlier version of Mary while Horus is frequently compared to Jesus.

Conspiracy buffs would claim the link between the pagan goddess and the modern day Islamists is intended. Sceptics would call it coincidence. I just find it interesting.

So we're back to sun gods again, and the many similarities between the various belief systems – Christian, Jewish, Muslim, pagan and others. The same roots? – I'd say so.

And when it comes to the *Da Vinci Code*, Dan Brown cleverly brings together various religious and bloodline theories in a first class thriller that really makes you think.

He links ideas of the divine feminine to a story about an old royal bloodline running through Jesus and surviving to this day. The implication is that Christianity's focal character survived crucifixion to marry and have children with Mary Magdalene.

Many consider this blasphemy. I think the jury's still out.

And of course the idea of 13 all-important bloodlines running through human history and constantly being in control dovetails for some into the New World Order issue.

Is the NWO a good or bad thing? Ah, there's the rub.

To my knowledge, three former US presidents have used the phrase in speeches – Republicans George H W Bush and his son, George W Bush, plus Democrat Bill Clinton. So have other leading US politicians.

This side of the pond, Tony Blair, Gordon Brown and David Cameron have all employed the phrase.

In all these cases, it was painted as a good move – a unifying initiative bringing peace and harmony, preventing a repeat of the two world wars.

If only this were true, I'd be all for it, as I said a few paragraphs ago. But critics warn that it could mean an oppressive and savage regime where the privileged few controlled the rest of us, treating us as little more than slaves. I fear they're right.

There would be world government, religion, army and bank. And we'd all be micro chipped and linked to a global computer system, ending up as little more than remote-controlled flesh and blood robots, say the idea's vehement opponents.

I accept that having your ID details and medical records stored on a silicon chip somewhere on or in your body could have distinct advantages if you're in an accident or a crisis where fast identification is vital.

But what other information could these chips contain – and how could it be used against us? That's the chilling question. And one that needs to be answered before we go down that road.

Some argue that the two global wars last century were both about stopping a despotic hostile takeover, and yet that's exactly what we're allowing to happen now.

Nazi Germany and Communist Russia were nothing compared to what's coming, an Earth-spanning version of both, claim these seriously alarmed people.

And it's coming in stages through the use of unelected secretive bodies such as the Bilderberg Group, Trilateral Commission, the Council on Foreign Relations and the Round Table – the real seats of power where all the big decisions are made.

The politicians – some of them members, but many not – have to do what they're told and obey these decisions or be discredited and sidelined.

Secret societies such as the Freemasons are said to be key components in this initiative, but only at the highest levels with the vast majority of ordinary, decent members being kept unaware.

And there's also apparently outlandish allegations of top America politicians, business leaders and showbiz stars taking part in bizarre dark rituals annually at Bohemian Grove, a 2,700-acre campground in California.

And of course similar strange and seemingly Satanic rituals at Yale University's hall called the Tomb, housing the secretive Skull and Bones Society.

Father and son ex-presidents Bush and current US Secretary of State John Kerry have all been named as attendees.

Oh, and the society's sinister skull and bones crest carries the strange number 322. Conspiracy theorists point out that the Brussels terrorist attacks came on March 22.

Coincidence? Most probably, but in this smoke and mirrors reality, who can say?

A favourite tactic of the NWO brigade is apparently the false flag operation – organising, orchestrating or allowing a crisis or terrorist attack to happen and then making sure it's blamed on another group they want to turn people violently against.

It's certainly true that there are many gaping holes in the official account of the 911 atrocities in America, as if lie has followed lie, the blame's been misdirected and a massive cover-up has taken place.

And look at film footage of the politicians' own changing versions of the weapons of mass destruction claims against Iraq, a country bombed and invaded as a result of 911 in the total absence of any concrete proof that it was in any way involved.

Afghanistan was also ravaged – again, with no evidence of involvement in 911 – on the premise that Osama bin Laden, alleged mastermind behind the attacks, was hiding there. But the allies were apparently unable to find him in caves built with CIA cash.

And bin Laden was already on an FBI most wanted list years before the twin towers mass murders. A CNN television news team managed to track down a feller named as him who they then proceeded to interview in 1997, four years before 911.

Osama seemingly had business links with the Bushes. Oh, and apparently members of his own family were allowed to fly out of America with other Saudis just days after the atrocities, even though airspace was shut down. So he was really hard to find!

Just to emphasize, I'm no lover of bin Laden or Saddam Hussein any more than I am of Islamic State, Adolf Hitler or Joseph Stalin. They've all been equally despicable.

I abhor vicious individuals, murderous nutters and oppressive regimes of all kinds.

I'm merely saying that it's never that clear cut and our political leaders are just as likely to lie to us, exploit us and sanction abominable behaviour as their opponents.

At the end of the day we're told all sorts of things and we have to make up our own minds what we think is true and false – or, more accurately, what our hearts tell us is.

Incidentally, the United Nations, with its so-called peace-keeping military section, is viewed as an ideal vehicle for transition to the world government and army.

The UN Security Council has five permanent members – the USA, France, the UK, Russia and China. Notice no Germany, Italy, Spain, Canada, Australia or Japan, although they've all been temporary members.

And when people say part of the master plan is a single world currency, they mean credit that can be awarded or withdrawn at will. Notes and coins will no longer exist.

Former Democrat US President John F Kennedy issued a warning about secret societies in a speech he gave in April 1961.

This is what he said:

"The very word "secrecy" is repugnant in a free and open society; and we are as a people inherently and historically opposed to secret societies, to secret oaths and secret proceedings.

"We decided long ago that the dangers of excessive and unwarranted concealment of pertinent facts far outweighed the dangers which are cited to justify it."

A bit later in the same speech he referred to:

"A monolithic and ruthless conspiracy that relies on covert means for expanding its sphere of influence – on infiltration instead of invasion, on subversion instead of elections, on intimidation instead of free choice, on guerrillas by night instead of armies by day."

And look what happened to him – shot dead in Dallas, Texas, in November 1963.

While writing that little lot, I've been also been thoroughly relishing the superb sounds of The Levellers, Blur and Donovan.

I've also revisited the great Marianne Faithfull album Broken English and the sublime Selling England by the Pound by Genesis. Sweet!

****

CHAPTER FOUR – FEAR AND LOVE

April 6 – Some readers might well doubt or disagree with much of what I've said in this book and my earlier ones.

It's crazy talk, literally unbelievable, they could assert, asking the obvious question of why the heck our leaders would want to treat us so shabbily. What's their motive?

Well here's two strong ones – gaining more wealth and power. Inciting trouble and causing sharp divisions in society keeps the callous elite firmly in the driving seat, plus it's good for business. War is the most lucrative activity of all – for the bankers.

And fortunes can be made selling weaponry to combatants and rebuilding shattered countries after conflicts. These are indisputable facts.

But it's not all hopeless. Rays of optimism can and do pierce the gathering gloom. I'm with David Icke – the future IS starting to look brighter as more and more people wake up and see through the deceptions. Like him, I'm sure love will win in the end.

We gave our power away to these cruel control freaks and we can seize it back by refusing to buy into their falsehoods or accept their corrupt policies and actions.

Wise American comedian the late great Bill Hicks once said we face a simple choice between fear and love. I'm with love – every time!

The main top story on this morning's TV news concerns a fourth strike by junior doctors over the terms of new contracts being forced upon them by the government.

It's estimated that more than 5,000 operations will have to be postponed due to the 48-hour walkout that started at 8am.

Despicable scare-mongering politicians claim that people will die and a Department of Health official called the strike "irresponsible."

But the National Health Service and the British Medical Association say that the very regrettable action is due to the MPs' refusal to listen and negotiate. They add that it's more about patient safety than pay, and emergency operations will still be carried out – by other health professionals.

My admiration and support for our hard-pressed NHS is well known. I dedicated my book *Scalpels and Angels* to the nursing staff that looked after me when I was ill with my heart crisis.

And I'd much rather align myself with dedicated care workers who could save lives than pampered out-of-touch callous clowns scoring political points at the expense of hospital staff and patients.

Rather than slate the strikers, Government ministers and their lackeys could stop the industrial action immediately – just by agreeing to hear the doctors out and reconsider the matter. But the bloody-minded buggers aren't going to are they?

I'm listening to one of the better albums from that whole punk/new wave era – Power in the Darkness by the Tom Robinson Band.

It's an often overlooked gem, just like the Boomtown Rats' debut 12-inch offering. But it's also scintillating rock, in TRB's case with potent, often politicized lyrics.

And hearing again Tom's song words, I get this overpowering feeling of déjà vu – he, too, was expressing rage at cold and cruel attitudes, just as I have a lot recently.

But it's interesting to note that, although Robinson hated Margaret Thatcher's right wing policies with a vengeance, it was actually Jim Callaghan's Labour in charge when the album first came out in 1978. Thatcher took over in May 1979.

Just goes to show that there's never been much difference between the two main parties when they've been in power, obeying a savagely conservative establishment.

Keeping with largely forgotten albums from the seventies, I've just finished Tom's and slapped on the Impossible Dream by the Sensational Alex Harvey Band (1974).

This brilliant group was criminally underrated full stop. I loved their punchy, highly inventive rock and roll with intriguing lyrics, performed with skill and flamboyance.

I saw both acts at Reading Festival (Alex 1977, Tom 1978) and both blew me away.

I'll never forget how Robinson totally won over the crowd, a large proportion of them macho, hairy, denim and leather hard rock fans, and got them to sing Glad to be Gay.

April 6, evening – Just watched an absorbing documentary called the Hidden Teachings of Jesus.

Basically, it maintained that Christianity's central character was actually a divinely-inspired guru and his oft-misunderstood sayings were in fact coded references to yoga – the path to enlightenment and the realization of the inner divinity we all possess.

Vivid picture language about Heaven, Hell and other concepts were in truth advice about how to use the practice to transcend the physical and reach a spiritual state.

And Jesus was just one of a line of humans, now ascended masters, who had shown us the means to do this, displaying great insight and wisdom that could liberate us all.

That might sound a bit fanciful but that's my fault. I'm attempting to pass on, in my own cack-handed style, ideas that made an awful lot of sense to me. The film makers expressed it all far more coherently, eloquently and convincingly than I ever could.

For example, they came up with a better version of my much-used isolated droplet of consciousness analogy, saying our own personal quota of consciousness was like sea water in a sealed bottle (the body), floating in the ocean it came from but separated from it until released back there. Brilliant!

Heaven was enlightenment touching divinity, reached by correct use of energy and the mind; Hell the flesh and blood container and its manufactured physical reality.

Check it out and you'll see what I mean. It's a practical guide to peace and love.

Of course, if we search too hard for truth we can end up being bombarded with all manner of convincing theories put forward by people extremely skilled in assembling facts and ideas so as to comply with their own views and agendas.

At the end of the day I guess we can only trust our hearts and instincts to tell us what rings true to us and what doesn't. In my case, much of the Jesus documentary did.

And let's face it, we all indulge in cruder forms of such information manipulation all the time in our faltering attempts to find sense in the mad world around us and make it fit our own paradigms and comfort zones.

April 7 – *The Hidden Teachings of Jesus* film ties in nicely with the mystical Gospel of Thomas, one of the ancient scriptures found at Nag Hammadi, Egypt, in 1945.

Buried in a sealed jar and discovered by a local farmer, the 12 leather-bound papyrus volumes contained 52 mostly Gnostic treatises, including some attributed to the apostles Philip and Peter and even Y'shua (Jesus) himself.

There are certain overlaps with the Bible scriptures but much of the material is distinctly different.

In the Gospel of Thomas, for example, Y'shua is quoted voicing some of the same advice, wisdom and parables also recounted in the New Testament. But the whole text is a more concentrated summary of His sayings with no narrative of His life story.

I'd argue this gives a far purer version of His spiritual teachings. Even better than John, the most mystical of the four Biblical gospels.

Indeed, the whole feel of the Thomas text veers much closer to Eastern religions than it does traditional Judaism.

It promotes meditation and contemplation, Oneness and the idea that we have divinity within us that we can access and develop should we choose to.

Heaven means opening ourselves to Oneness – universal eternal consciousness – while Hell is restricting ourselves inside the limits of physical reality. Both lie within us.

While accepting and embracing the physical, we should constantly strive for the spiritual, reflecting out the Holy Spirit that resides inside us all, says the text.

That way, we can each aspire to emulate the divinity-imbued Y'shua, who was symbolically born of the Holy Virgin – Mother Wisdom.

In other words, we can all realize our true potential as sons and daughters of the divine, loving parent.

Y'shua is quoted advising us to be "wise as serpents and innocent as doves."

This is interesting because it takes us back to the much-used serpent imagery. In other words, reptiles.

Take the Biblical Garden of Eden story, for example. The conventional interpretation is that Adam and Eve were punished for disobeying God, angering Him so much he banished them to a rough wilderness of sin and misery.

The Lord had told Adam he could eat the fruit of any tree except one. But the evil snake persuaded Eve to get Adam to eat an apple from it (have sex with her?).

As a result, they both realized they were naked and grabbed fig leaves to cover their embarrassment. They also gained worldly knowledge but incurred God's fury, becoming severed from the source of their own divinity, making them mortal.

But some claim this is a total reversal of the original message and in fact eating the apple from the Tree of Knowledge liberated the couple by making them wiser.

The serpent is often equated with the wicked fallen angel Satan, also called Lucifer – a very negative interpretation. But the term Lucifer is sometimes applied to the planet Venus – symbolising love – and the light you get from striking a match, both positive.

Satanists and other followers of Lucifer would thus argue that conventional thinking is therefore a total reversal of the truth, making them the advocates of illumination and wisdom while the God squad are actually the bad guys trying to hold us back.

The Gospel of Thomas quotation implies that there's a middle way employing the wisdom of the Earth-bound snake, representing physicality, and the skyward-soaring dove, a widely-used symbol for spirituality.

Spirit is eternal and death a transition to another state of being. Jesus is even quoted in the Bible as saying "before Abraham was, I am."

But there's a stark warning about allowing a fractured physical reality at war with itself to dominate our thoughts at the expense of our spiritual essences, and especially letting our egos to run amok – a sure fire way to incur pain and misery – Hell.

Returning to our friend the Eden snake, that I see symbolising the dangerously unfettered ego and the flaws and limitations of the physical, I find it fascinating that serpents and reptiles are a recurring theme in myths spanning the globe and history.

Indeed, ancient civilisations in India, China, Peru, Mexico, Egypt and many other times and places claimed to be descended from reptilian, serpent or lizard beings that came down from the stars to breed with our ancestors.

There are even references to this in the Old Testament (Genesis, Isaiah and Ezekiel).

Of course, these are evocative legends, but is there any underlying truth? The constant references to the sun, serpents, spaceships and stars in texts and artwork – even cave drawings dating back many thousands of years – makes me wonder.

The accurate knowledge displayed in ancient documents about our universe, cutting edge technology, the Earth's geography and intricate medical procedures certainly suggests there was once an advanced but now lost civilisation – Atlantis.

Some say it was wiped out in a cataclysm and we're only now once again reaching the same levels of sophistication existing before the world was plunged into ignorance.

Odd-shaped human like skulls, the portrayals of flying saucers in centuries-old pictures and the sheer volume of reported UFO sightings in more recent times also point to an alien connection.

And this in turn brings us back to the ruling bloodlines theory linking Egypt, Europe and our own monarchs through the ages – and the reptilian alien DNA allegations.

It's interesting to note that royals and aristocrats are sometimes called blue bloods.

April 7, several hours later – To return to the topic of information about Y'shua and his disciples not included in authorized versions of the Bible.

The Gospel of Philip, another Nag Hammadi text, mentions the close relationship between Y'shua and Mary Magdalene, largely ignored in the New Testament as we know it. (This seems to be supported by the separately-discovered Gospel of Mary).

Other documents found at Nag Hammadi have titles including the Secret Book of James, the Gospel of Truth, the Treatise on the Resurrection, the Apocryphon of John, the Gospel of the Egyptians, the Sophia of Jesus Christ, the Apocalypse of Paul and the Interpretation of Knowledge.

Then there's the Dead Sea Scrolls unearthed between 1946 and 1956, a collection of 981 different texts found in eleven caves in the immediate vicinity of the ancient settlement at Khirbet, Qumran, Israel.

Many of the writings from these two locations appear to contradict or raise doubts about important aspects of the Bible story.

There's even a Gospel of Peter – Jesus' main man according to Christian tradition, famously referred to as the rock on which He built His church. Bearing that in mind, you'd think this text would be an obvious inclusion in the Bible. So why isn't it?

All the documents I've referred to have been authenticated but none have subsequently been incorporated into the New Testament. Again, I wonder why.

Who's to say what actually is an accurate account of the life and sayings of Y'shua and his apostles and what isn't? It's a mind bender for sure. No wonder some folk just sidestep the whole lot, choosing to be non-believers or find other faiths to adopt.

Another very interesting point is that some atheists believe in life after death. This appears to fly in the face of the old God versus oblivion argument beloved of many.

But if you think about it why should this be paradoxical? All it does is show that more people are realizing it's not just a choice of two rival options – religion or atheism.

It's just been presented that way for far too long to cause splits and conflict, a huge part of the game plan being masterminded by those in the know and in charge.

As always, we need to consider all possibilities. Accept no-one's take on the truth at face value. Documents and artwork can be forged, facts manipulated and history altered frighteningly easily. Keep that mind open and listen to your heart.

All this stuff really does appeal big time to the ageing hippy in me. But please rest assured I won't be off to the shops any time soon to invest in any bells, kaftans, Afghan coats or gaudy, ridiculously flared trousers.

Granted, I'm a firm advocate of peace and love and that whole sixties vibe. I do burn incense sticks and like to wear bead necklaces and bracelets. And I did recently purchase a couple of cheap second hand but I think stylish hats. But that's about it.

How appropriate it is that at present I'm alternating my computer background wallpaper between striking photos of Stonehenge and the Giza Pyramids.

Which reminds me – pyramids and standing stone circles can also be found all over the world, another indicator of common religious themes spanning time and cultures.

I've just had a thought. Millions of people have been tortured, beheaded, drawn and quartered, crucified and burnt to death over the centuries simply for voicing worldviews different from their societies' savagely enforced belief systems.

Thank goodness that's no longer the case –well, at least not here at present!

I'm revelling in my enthusiastically revived quest for truth and spirituality after my recent half-year excursion into the realms of romantic love with all that entailed.

Okay, it ended in tears but it was a scintillating adventure while it lasted. And it did make me aware that there's life in this old dog yet and I can still have a sexual relationship combining the finer spiritual and physical aspects of human existence.

Those two aspects are interlinked and interlocked, but I had thought the couple option was now beyond me. I've realized otherwise to my great surprise, elation and relief.

So, while determined not to get too distracted again from one of my two main purposes (learning and sharing) I am kinda missing the company of a lady friend. I'd got so used to managing without it that I'd forgotten how flipping great it feels.

After the heartbreak, devastation and raw emotion phase, I'm once again yearning for the female touch and influence in both my days and nights. And that's a good thing.

I have Paula to thank for that.

Oh, and just in case you were wondering – Chemical Brothers, Robert Miles and Dreadzone.

April 8 – Spaceships and aliens, pyramids and Satanists, hidden messages and human sacrifices. I suppose we might as well chuck in ghosts and crop circles, wizards and dragons. Welcome to La La Land.

Actually, there is a school of thought that reported modern UFO and alien sightings are merely updated versions of the many accounts of ghosts and goblins in bygone times – mankind's feeble attempts to grasp and convey the inexplicable.

I guess we all have to ask ourselves the very pertinent question – if we were convinced we'd seen a UFO or ghost, would we keep quiet through fear of what others might think, or blurt it out and risk being derided and ridiculed?

Magic as I understand it – as opposed to clever sleight of hand or illusion weaving – is the skill to influence objects and energies using the power of the human mind.

This skill is sometimes called wizardry and its use can be either positive and helpful or negative and harming – hence the terms black and white magic. Healers can also use natural energies to good effect.

As for dragon references, these are similar to the widely-used snake and lizard symbolism. The word is sometimes employed to describe important bloodlines and also the significant energy lines running across the Earth's surface.

All this stuff is intriguingly interwoven through human cultures and history. I'm lucky to have the opportunity to look into it all in my quest to find the truth.

I'm stuck in this crazy reality whether I like it or not. And it does have its advantages. But I don't accept it, not any more. It's so sad that most people are so busy handling its complex manifestations they have little or no time to consider the bigger picture.

The way I see it, the trick is to be in the world but not of it. We are shackled to conventional reality while we're conscious, only shaking free in dreams and death.

So use it to your own advantage but retain your integrity and stop buying into it.

Look at the Beatles. They had their minds blown wide open by drink, drugs and religion and never thought the same again.

Some might argue that Paul McCartney later sold out big style by becoming a multi-millionaire and accepting a knighthood.

I suppose you could say the same about Mick Jagger, lead singer with the original bad boy rebel band the Rolling Stones.

But I prefer to see it as them seriously taking the piss – out of the system, not us – while never truly succumbing to the bullshit. Fair play to the pair of them I say.

And I'd point out that they've entertained and inspired countless legions of people across the world and raised shed loads of cash for worthy causes, unlike other selfish, ruthless establishment leeches who have made fortunes by viciously exploiting others.

Enlightened masters taught that there were several ways to escape this messed up, damaging reality and access our higher selves.

Y'shua (Jesus) was one of these, although it's not mentioned much in the authorized Bible, where he's painted as the one true Lord, at one with God.

I maintain that he was actually born a human being but reached a supreme level of spiritual enlightenment through acquired knowledge and strict self-discipline.

He developed his own inner divinity to the point that he was imbued with it and it positively shone from him. He became a great healer, saint like, angel like, a holy man and great teacher of divine wisdom.

But he said we could all emulate his achievements with the right skills and attitude. His actual words are recorded as:

Verily, verily, I say unto you, He that believeth on me, the works that I do shall he do also; and greater works than these shall he do; because I go unto my Father.

John 14:12, King James Bible

Yoga, vigorous exercise and meditation are among the more extreme ways of achieving peace of mind, mental and physical health and enlightenment.

But I adopt the lazy man's methods to acquire much milder and less concentrated versions – reading, watching, learning, short scenic walks and quiet contemplation.

Meanwhile, control freaks acting like scumbags screw us at every turn in their mad drive to amass and keep wealth and power for themselves.

They create problems, get the desired reactions from us and then come up with the solutions they had up their sleeves all along.

Manufactured crises are presented as isolated incidents so we don't catch on that they're all part of the master plan.

We are presented with an illusion of democracy while unelected bureaucrats govern more and more aspects of our lives.

Dark overlords working from the shadows seem hell bent on destroying all countries and religions as they merge a shrinking number of power blocks into one centralised dictatorship backed up by a single unit of credit administered by a world bank.

Freedom will go and stringent laws will be enforced by one huge army whose only enemy will be anyone daring to step out of line and not do as they're told.

Fears of pandemics will be the excuse for injecting us all with mind altering drugs or liberty-robbing microchips under the guise of mass vaccination.

Our food, water supplies and medications will be increasingly used to mess with our minds and bodies.

Economies will be deliberately crashed as Israel, Russia, China and North Korea are all used to set nation against nation until none are left.

Really? Well, that's what David Icke and others would have us believe.

It's a nightmare scenario for sure. Could any of it happen? Sceptics will say no, absolutely not. Our politicians would never allow it.

But I say yes, terrifyingly, it could all come to pass thanks to people's smug complacency that's already letting it. It doesn't have to end in disaster though.

The more individuals that stand up and say no, enough is enough, we're seizing back the power we gave you and will no longer co-operate with your mad policies, the less likely any of it will become. Peaceful resistance is well overdue. It's still not too late.

Good grief! Methinks it's time for a quick strum on the ol' geetar.

I've been typing away to the music of Paul Weller, Pulp and Focus writing this entry.

April 8, 11pm – Just had a great time with people who mean a lot to me, namely Sam Excell, Carl Young, Rudy, Bailey, Jem Hannen, Rich Jeffery, Rebecca Hall, Joedie Watt and the dogs Albert and Bramble. On the way home, I got a Chinese takeaway.

I learned from a poster in the shop that, according to the Chinese zodiac, I was born in a year of the horse (1954), making me warm hearted, with lots of friends, but spendthrift and lacking persistence.

All true, as it goes, but I prefer our conventional sun sign zodiac definition, by which as a Piscean I'm imaginative, accepting and devoted but also over sensitive, lazy, indecisive and escapist. That's me in a nutshell.

April 9 – God, the One, Supreme Consciousness is about unity not division and exists beyond the polarities of positive and negative, black and white, male and female and so on. Without the dark, we couldn't appreciate the light, warmth would mean nothing without the cold and we require both sunshine and rain to survive.

These polarities need each other as much as we need them. We should aim to balance, not eliminate. The positive should control the negative, light overpower the dark and warmth dominate the cold while male and female energies work as equal partners.

This is the way forward to peace and harmony, love, enlightenment and bliss. That's what I think anyway.

April 10 – Last night in the Bell was another good one, with John Palmer, Ben Avill, Jenny Daniels, John Gaynor, Jem Hannen, Stuart and Melody Moss, Ollie Okoye, Penny Williams (briefly) and guv'nors Laura Williams and Mark Evans.

Plus Jim, another mate who used to be a barman there. Don't know his surname.

I had a fascinating conversation with Ben, a guy less than half my age, about music and especially the Beatles, Chuck Berry and Billy Joel. Cool as a cucumber, man.

As I write, this, I'm enjoying Queen Rocks – a compilation of the kick ass harder stuff that I love that eschews the glossy pop-opera songs I'm not too keen on.

In the news, more than 100 people have died in a temple fire in South India after firecrackers caused a massive blast.

And David Cameron's in hot water over tax-avoiding offshore funds. He's not done anything illegal but he's being called greedy, insensitive and an outrageous hypocrite after chiding others for doing much the same while cutting citizens' vital cash funds.

Some critics have even demanded he resign.

By the way, tax avoidance is allowed so long as you're honest about it. Tax evasion is deliberate deception – fraud – and most certainly is against the law.

I've just been thinking about us all having lighter and darker aspects.

You can't just take the good bits of someone, pretending their bad traits don't exist – to try to will always end in tears.

April 11 – I'm sat here at my computer with one of those 24-hour blood pressure monitors attached to me. I went to the clinic at Shelley Road, Boscombe, at 9.30 this morning to have it fitted and I'm due to return at 9.30 tomorrow to have it removed.

An inflating sleeve like the ones used in surgeries and hospitals stays wrapped around my upper arm with a tube running from it to the monitor device clipped to my belt that takes a reading every half hour during the day and each hour at night.

It's one of those things I have to do once a year now at my doctor's request.

But returning to what I was saying a while earlier about Jesus being born human – and also in light of the biological impossibility of his mother Mary being literally a virgin, there are baffling references in the Bible and elsewhere to the Lord having siblings.

Matthew and Mark both mention four brothers, named as James, Joses (or Joseph), Judas and Simon. Mark refers to sisters without identifying them or giving a number.

Clergymen are quick to point out that Joseph (as in Holy Mother Mary's husband) is reputed to have been older than Her and previously married to someone else, making it perfectly possible that he had children, Y'shua's (Jesus') step siblings.

But The Bible simply refers to brothers and sisters without specifying one way or the other, leading us the wonder whether at least some of them were Mary's children, younger than the Lord and born the usual way.

Some texts speak of James being Y'shua's older brother (making it more likely he was Joseph's but not Mary's), and of his being the very first Bishop of Jerusalem.

It's also widely held that John the Baptist was a cousin. He was certainly considered important enough to baptize Y'shua in the River Jordan.

Whatever the true nature of the family ties, it's crystal clear to me that all these people, and Mary Magdalene, were a lot closer to the Lord than convention suggests. They were most likely his inner circle and core members of the embryonic Church.

And yet they've all been largely airbrushed out of the picture, sidelined and neglected in the Christian Church that's been built up around the legends and legacies of the apostle Peter and Paul, who apparently only met Y'shua in visions. How strange!

Talk of the Lord having a brother called Judas reminds me of another mind-boggling assertion I read in a book some years ago – that Judas Iscariot was not only His brother, he was actually his twin!

Others don't go this far but do similarly advocate that rather than being the villain of the piece, Judas was in fact a close and trusted companion – so trusted he was the one chosen by Jesus himself to turn him in to the authorities so he could fulfil his destiny.

While we're on the subject of Y'shua, he's said to have been capable of some pretty amazing feats – walking on water, raising people from the dead, curing the blind and lame, casting out demons, turning water into wine and weird stuff like that.

These accounts could be deep, rich symbolism – like the virgin birth and death on the cross references – or simply crude attempts to explain the wondrous achievements of a spiritually advanced, divinity-imbued person apparently able to perform miracles.

What was I saying about the wise and skilled being able to manipulate objects and energies to certain ends? Mind over matter and use of magic can appear miraculous.

We're back to that word again – miracles. But my definition of the term is those beautiful, heart-warming, life-affirming surprises than can happen once in a while.

As for water into wine, I recently heard one Biblical scholar speculate that it could be allegorical – Jesus representing the rain that fell on the vineyard, nurturing the grapes used to make the wine. Sounds as good an explanation as any.

Don't forget, wine was a crucial sustenance in those days before water purification and sewerage systems were in common usage.

And Jesus is called the Son of Man as well as the Son of God. I'd suggest He was both at the same time, born of human beings but imbued with an advanced level of divinity emanating from the One and operating through his exceptional higher self.

Some link Y'shua with a royal bloodline running through Egyptian Pharaohs, Him and his (hotly disputed) children with Mary Magdalene to end up flowing through the European Merovingian monarchs.

From there it survived over the centuries to the present day and the Merovingians' descendents including our own current Queen and leading figures like the Bushes, it's alleged. Hey, we're back to the ruling bloodlines theory again!

Been listening to Eminem, Cream, the Ramones and Crowded House.

April 12 – Went back to the clinic today to have the blood pressure gizmo taken off.

The print-out showed my readings were a bit higher than last year's but the nurse said mine tended to be on the low side anyway so it wasn't a cause for concern –yet.

That's why I take a beta blocker pill daily – to keep the BP down and stop my heart getting too agitated.

Now I need to get my annual blood test arranged at my local surgery and make an appointment to see Dr Mitchell to discuss the results of that and the BP monitor info.

I've got the live Muse album Haarp on at the moment. What a great rock band!

I'm off in a while to meet Paula for a few drinks at the Bell. But first I think I'll draw this section of my life journal to a close.

To sum up the religious and ideological matters I've been writing about, the way I see it, God is Allah is Jah is Jehovah; Jesus equates to Krishna, Muhammad and Meher Baba, the Holy Spirit is chi is prana and so on.

And Oneness, the Supreme Consciousness, is all, incorporating unity, harmony, peace and love.

Yes, at the end of the day it all boils down to love. No matter how you perceive the great creative force often labelled God.

We've all heard the old chestnut – if God is so loving, why does He permit bad things to happen? This is a childish question revealing a very simplistic view, a crude bid to cop out big time by pushing responsibility for all the world's ills onto a remote entity.

Newsflash – unfortunate accidents and fallible humans cause tragedy and suffering.

God isn't some white bearded old guy sat in a gold and diamond throne in the sky, nor a spiteful bad-tempered vengeful parent condemning sinful non-believes to Hell.

God equals love and embraces the whole of existence, including our own higher selves – the more positive and caring aspects of our individual sparks of Consciousness or drops from the Great Ocean, however you wish to see it.

Either way, the whole seriously misunderstood concept is a lot more subtle and complex than many unthinking, lazy picture language addicts try to maintain.

I fully accept that people will have their own ideas on such matters. Some might passionately disagree with what I've written, saying I've got it all wrong.

But that's the way I choose to see things at present. I might alter my views or certain parts of them tomorrow or some time in the future. Like everyone, I reserve that right.

And here's a thing – atheists and agnostics can be good or bad just like anyone else. Tolerate and respect each others' views. Agree to differ without falling out with anyone.

Spread the love girls and boys. There's too much hurt in this world, don't add to it.

End of Part One

****

HUMOUR AND MIRACLES

Part Two

April and May 2016

CHAPTER FIVE – TYPING TO GREAT TUNES

April 13 – Well, Paula and I did indeed meet up at the Bell yesterday (a Tuesday, her usual day off from work). Very pleasant it was too.

We had a nice chinwag, a few laughs and saw and chatted to guv'nors Laura and Mark, their adorable puppy dog Flick and a barman called Dave.

I went to my doctor's surgery this morning to book my blood test there for a week today and my appointment to see my GP Dr Tim Mitchell the following Tuesday.

I'm enjoying Ozzy Osbourne's classic Blizzard of Oz album as I write.

Earlier I was listening to Alice Cooper's excellent Welcome to My Nightmare Two – a Christmas present from Paula.

She and I share an admiration for these two heavy rockers – in fact they're her two favourite music stars. She loves heavy metal in general and Ozzy's group Black Sabbath in particular. One of my Christmas presents to her was a Sabbath tattoo.

(Another of her festive gifts to me was a striking leather and metal bracelet that I love and wear a lot. She noticed I had it on yesterday and commented on the fact).

It's interesting to note that I'd put both Alice and Ozzy on my list of artists I wanted to listen to again three days ago – before I even knew I was going to see my treasured female pal yesterday. What do they say about great minds thinking alike?

April 14 – Over the past couple of days, the BBC television news has been dominated by what I see as a total non-story.

It concerns the fact that Culture Secretary John Whittingdale dated a sex worker a couple of years ago. So ruddy what!

A Downing spokesman said quite rightly that Mr Whittingdale, 56, is a single man entitled to a private life.

The MP has defended himself by pointing out that he didn't know the woman was an escort when he met her through an online dating site – and he ended their relationship on finding out. Plus it all happened before he was appointed as a government minister.

I can't see what all the fuss is about; especially bearing in mind there's no shortage of genuine news stories to be covered.

So long as it doesn't affect the way he does his job or make him vulnerable to undue pressure or blackmail, why on Earth should it be made into such a big deal?

It's not an issue for me and shouldn't be for anyone else. The only problem I have with Mr Whittingdale is that he's a member of a disgraceful government.

I'm sure there's lots of real dirt to be dug concerning these dreadful people, their outrageously unfair and unjust policies, their cruelty, deception and hypocrisy.

But no, our good old media is, as usual, so obsessed with sex it would rather go with a titillating non-story than tackle proper issues and ask probing questions about things that really matter because they affect us all.

Flippin' 'eck! No wonder society's so hung up on sex in general and sexual deviance in particular when its spoon fed this sort of salacious trivia daily by a sick and twisted Press that in all other respects is the system's pathetically compliant PR division.

I've just had the magnificent Nirvana on my CD player. It was fabulous – feeding the classic trio's music through my stereo system to create a truly wonderful sound.

Now I'm typing away to the Sex Pistols' debut album Never Mind the Bollocks.

Oh, and after writing yesterday's journal entry, I put on an album by the impressive Marillion (with Fish). Great prog rock with interesting and poetic lyrics.

April 15 – Happy 50th birthday Chris Davis. He and his lovely wife Louise are a really nice couple. I attended their wedding a few years ago and have been to a couple of their excellent New Year's Eve parties – December 31st is Lou's birthday.

I've mentioned Chris and Lou a few times in my earlier books.

I have Screamadelica on my stereo system as I bash away at my computer keyboard. It really is a mighty fine album by festival favourites dance/rock band Primal Scream.

Earlier on, I was immersing myself in the heavy glam sound of the Darkness.

Yesterday I ended up finishing my CD playing session with the Best of the Smiths. Marvellous!

April 16 – And happy birthday Rich Jeffery. I saw him yesterday (Friday) evening at Sam Excell's and we had a few celebratory drinks in the company of Carl Young, Jem Hannen, Tina Mcauley and others.

April 16, 6pm – Just had a very sweet surprise – Phil brought Chloe over to see me (Emily was at home with Lucas, who had fallen asleep, and Harvey was out with Em's parents).

It was lovely seeing my son and granddaughter again, but doubly so when he told me the main reason for their visit – to bring me a computer he no longer needed for work.

It's a better, more up to date and faster one than I had been using for a few years. Phil kindly set it up for me and I'm using it now to write this using Microsoft Word.

April 18 – At least 272 people have been confirmed dead and more than 1,500 injured after Ecuador was hit by its most powerful earthquake in decades,

Some 10,000 troops and 3,500 police are being deployed in the affected areas as rescue operations continue.

The magnitude 7.8 quake struck on Saturday evening. We all feel for those poor traumatized and grieving people.

It follows two powerful quakes in Japan last week that between them killed 42 people. A quarter of a million residents there have been told to leave their homes amid fears of further violent tremors.

AFC Bournemouth lost 2-1 at home yesterday (Sunday) to Liverpool but it looks like the Cherries are going to survive their first season in the Premier League and be there for another one at least.

Absolutely brilliant! I'm chuffed to bits. Well done manager Eddie Howe and the lads – you've done your town and all its residents proud!

Last night I was in the Bell with managers Laura Williams and Mark Evans, bar manager Nicola Williams, her feller Mark, Matt Brant, John Gaynor, regulars Brian and Darren and Simon "Squeak" Turnbull.

As usual on a Sunday, it was karaoke. And deejay Ross Maslin played his customary mix of old school dance floor classic tracks from the eighties and nineties. Sweet!

As I write, I'm playing Bruce Springsteen – appropriately nicknamed the Boss.

A bit earlier, I thoroughly enjoyed REM's outstanding album Life's Rich Pageant. It was actually their fourth but the one I heard first and it blew me away. Over the weekend I've also listened to Slade, Camel and Rage Against the Machine.

In Camel's case, I loved once again hearing their concept album the Snow Goose, a modern musical masterpiece in the same class as Mike Oldfield's Tubular Bells.

Both still give me that shiver up and down the spine which all the best music does – no matter how many times I hear it.

April 19 – The death toll in the Ecuador earthquake is said to have risen to 413. And at least 21 people have been wounded in a bomb blast on a bus in Jerusalem, according to local police.

Over the past six months, 29 Israelis have been killed in a wave of stabbings, shootings and car-ramming attacks blamed on Palestinians or Israeli Arabs.

About 200 Palestinians – mostly attackers, according to Israel – have been killed in that period.

Israel, Libya, Syria, Iraq, Iran – have you noticed how most of the violence and deaths in the Middle East are occurring in places mentioned in the Bible and the accepted cradles of ancient civilisations? I'd suggest this is no fluke but totally intentional.

Aggressive forces invading and plundering these areas – whether Islamic State, American and British troops or whoever – have apparently destroyed many sacred texts and other precious and highly informative ages-old documents.

This is a vicious, cold-blooded tactic to rob communities and individuals of their cultures, religions, ideologies and senses of origin, identity and nationhood, enforcing on them alternative worldviews in the invaders' own images – thus rewriting history.

Events like 911, the London Bombs and the killing sprees in Paris and Brussels are blamed on certain extremist groups and then used as reasons to devastate lands, kill thousands of civilians and imposing new regimes compliant to Western ambitions.

Or rather, the ambitions of a rich and powerful elite relentlessly advancing its own agenda for world domination using sincere warriors on all sides as cannon fodder.

I feel the conflicts in Afghanistan, the Ukraine and other flashpoint sites are also connected to this millennia-old ideological war engineered by these brutes.

There's nothing new here – Hitler's armed forces and those of the Allies fighting them were similarly manipulated to indiscriminately bomb, attack, kill and maim.

Geneva Convention? – I would laugh out loud, but it's no laughing matter. War has no sodding rules.

But such-and-such organisation claimed responsibility for this or that terrorist attack, some would say. How do we know? – Just because we're told it don't make it true.

I'll emphasize yet again that I'm no apologist for any violent grouping inflicting death and injury, especially on the innocent. They're all as sick in the head as each other.

This includes any ideological extremist and those in military uniforms of all kinds. The twisted leaders that is, not the thousands of loyal, decent, patriotic or religiously sincere followers conned into believing they're doing the right thing.

And conned by despicable creatures that don't give a damn about them and will throw them on the scrap heap as soon as they've served their purpose, leaving them physically or mentally maimed, penniless, broken, disillusioned and sleeping rough.

Thank the stars for Homes for Heroes, Help for Heroes, the Royal British Legion and other charities and volunteers who have stepped in to do the friggin' government's job in looking after our ex-service personnel and their families. I salute and support them.

April 20, 8am – A car bomb in the Afghan capital Kabul has killed at least 28 people and wounded more than 300. What was I saying about Middle Eastern flash points?

I'm off to the surgery in a short while to have my annual blood check up with the nice but needle-wielding Nurse Maeve.

As it's a fasting blood test, I haven't eaten or drunk anything for nearly 12 hours, since 8.30 last night. Starving and thirsty, I'll have breakfast and take daily medications when I return home.

Stuff being staid and boring, I'd much rather grow old disgracefully!

April 20, 11am – I've been to the surgery, popped back home for breakfast, been out again to the building society and then posted a letter. Now I'm back on the PC with a CD on the stereo system.

I'm savouring every moment of Jean Michel Jarre's quite splendid live album In Concert Houston/ Lyon. I could listen to this guy's music for hours. I could also listen to him talk about music for hours. He's a true artist, a poet and painter – using sound as his medium.

Next I'm going to slap on a disc by the superb Ozric Tentacles, then a bit of Rush.

Yesterday I once again got into two other very good long players – Demon Days by the Gorillaz and Trans-Europe Express by Kraftwerk.

April 20, 7pm – Just heard on the TV news that funny woman Victoria Wood died earlier today following a short battle with cancer. She was 62 – same age as I am.

Victoria was a brilliant comedy writer and actor who could do stand-up, compose humorous songs and script classic telly shows such as *Acorn Antiques* and *Dinner Ladies*. She deservedly won five Baftas and her demise is a huge loss to showbiz.

April 21 – Happy fifth birthday to my grandson Lucas Money. Hope it's lovely.

It's also the Queen's 90th, making her our oldest as well as longest-reigning monarch ever. Beacons are being lit and parties held all over the world to mark the occasion.

We're watching history being made but I can't get too excited about it. I have nothing against the Royals as people and I accept that their positions mean they work hard and have little time off or privacy. But they spearhead an unjust, elitist system I detest.

Does this make unpatriotic? Absolutely not! I love England and the democratic ideals most of us yearn to see in our precious country. I never want to leave these shores.

Listening to Pink's good album Missundaztood while prattling on here.

I've previously bemoaned the forced split of science from spirituality centuries ago – and I've welcomed the enlightened move to reunite them now in progress.

I myself have fallen into the trap of segregating the creativity and artistry I so admire from the mathematics and logic I find can be cold and soulless.

But our wise ancestors, back through the mists of time, knew they were totally complementary, linked in a quite beautiful whole.

Post-Einstein cutting-edge technologists in fields such noetics science and quantum physics are coming to the same conclusions as mystics always have.

Apparently solid matter, the basis of our whole five-sense reality, is made up of atoms, which are themselves largely empty space. Most of our DNA is called "junk" because no-one's yet worked out its purpose.

We only use a tiny fraction of our brainpower. And the Universe is 85 per cent dark matter that's a complete mystery to us.

All these are facts confirmed by the men and women in white lab coats. Just imagine if we could ascertain how to utilize all those huge gaps in our seriously flawed reality.

Humankind would make a sensational evolutionary leap, hopefully towards spirituality and a new appreciation of our untapped inner divinity.

I'm not alone in thinking this big change has already begun. I'm also convinced that throughout history certain people have been able to access the wisdom our ancient ancestors had and the power they exercised before humanity's forced plunge into darkness and ignorance.

(That plunge has been portrayed in various ways including the Biblical Flood, mankind's fall from grace, the banishment from Eden and the destruction of Atlantis.)

The massive problem is that often these individuals have been motivated by the malevolent negative side of Consciousness and used their acquired knowledge and the inborn skills we all have to cruel and selfish ends at others peoples' expense.

Only a handful have been guided by the positive – and these we call gurus, adepts, masters, teachers, prophets and visionaries. Some have founded the great religions.

I've always considered mathematics dull, boring and tedious. I've had little interest and lacked ability, feeling far more at home in the imaginative, creative, artistic field.

But I've learned some new things of late that have changed my view quite radically.

Things about the golden ratio and the Fibonacci Sequence.

(Yes I'm currently reading the *Da Vinci Code* – but I've researched this further and it's all provable fact).

The Fibonacci Sequence is 0, 1, 2,3,5,8,13,21,34 and so on, each number being the sum total of the previous two.

It's tied in with the golden ratio, 1.618 – and the two together crop up time and time again throughout human history and the natural world.

The Egyptians used them in constructing the Giza Pyramids, they can be found in the dimensions of centuries-old buildings and mosaics, the artwork of Freemasons' temples, the music of Beethoven and Mozart and Leonardo Da Vinci's paintings.

Did these people know this, was it pure instinct, an unrecognized memory of past wisdom buried in the collective subconscious – or just fluke? Whichever the case, it's a fascinating fact.

And I like to think that, whether consciously conceived or not, the numerous and diverse repetitions of these mathematical concepts is no coincidence.

It's long been recognized that so-called sacred geometry and numerology – using the power of numbers – are both divinely-inspired.

The Fibonacci sequence and golden ratio can be found in flower petals, sea shells, pine cones, hurricanes, spiral galaxies, human hands and faces and even DNA molecules. Amazing, innit?

So the Great Divine Consciousness – God – is a mathematical genius?

I would have taken a lot more interest if this is how maths had been taught at school. But that's the point I guess – places of so-called learning are nothing of the kind.

All they are there for is getting students to pass exams by repeating back whatever they're told without too much questioning or expression of creative individuality.

The idea is to make them compliant slaves to the system, not troublesome free thinkers who can be a proper hindrance to its smooth running.

By the way, I've now got Frampton Comes Alive on the stereo – a monster of an album that's Bromley-born singer / songwriter / guitarist Peter Frampton at his best.

And while I'm on the subject of music – and having just mentioned Mozart and Beethoven – it's interesting to note (pun) that sound can create intriguing geometric patterns in sand or other particles as its frequencies are altered.

In fact, it can be used in a variety of ways to soothe, agitate or even break all manner of things from glass to human wills. It can be a great aid or a deadly weapon.

In the beginning was the Word, the Sound, the outward expression of the Thought, the Great Divine Consciousness – the Universal Creative Energy often called God.

Someone who's sexually aroused is said to be feeling horny. This is because horned gods and goddesses throughout cultures and history have been associated with sexual union and fertility – in both humans and nature.

Think about it – without such fertility we'd all be doomed, wouldn't we?

Indeed, religious rites and ceremonies the world over have and do incorporate the sex act, recognizing it as one way people can reach a state of divine bliss. Apparently, followers of the Jewish faith used to yonks ago before it became more conservative.

But when the Roman Catholic Church decided to demonize such ideas, and by association women, sex was suddenly seen as dirty and sinful outside marriage – and even within it unless it produced children.

So the horned and hoofed deities became linked with Satan as the Church tried to eliminate the feminine principle, creating a seriously lop-sided worldview reflected in societies across the globe – with devastating consequences.

The repression of perfectly normal, natural, healthy impulses has led to them breaking out in unhealthy, unnatural and abnormal ways through sexual deviance.

And the societies so hung up on such issues and responsible for this dreadful state of affairs then hypocritically meting out savage retribution for this type of behaviour.

Of course, sexual deviance is a very subjective concept indeed. Some still consider homosexuality and lesbianism types of perversion. I don't.

Others have a problem with older men dating considerably younger women, and vice versa. Although decidedly odd, I say why not? – just so long as the younger partner is above the age of consent of course.

Most of us would agree that child abuse is wrong – but some cultures even sanction that. And the age of consent varies from 14 to 18 depending on which country you're in.

I guess what I'm saying is we'd have far fewer problems with a more balanced societal view of all matters sexual.

April 21, 7pm – Good grief! Just heard on the news that pop superstar Prince has been found dead at his Paisley Park estate in Minnesota, USA. He was only 57.

It comes six days after he fell ill with what's been described as "severe flu."

The man who gave us Purple Rain was a highly influential performer and composer and many of his songs were covered by other artists.

One music reviewer once said that in concert, Prince "made Michael Jackson look nailed to the floor." I liked that. Sadly, he's now gone to meet Jackson in the afterlife.

April 22 – I've just lit a (purple) candle and I'm playing a Prince compilation CD as I write. All very appropriate bearing in mind his demise yesterday, but how well it fits in with what I'm about to say remains to be seen.

Striking a match is mostly seen as a positive gesture – to provide heat or light, cook food or something beneficial like that. But it could be used to ignite a dynamite fuse or spark an arson attack. And Lucifer (an archaic term for match) equates to Satan.

I feel this is an apt way to explain the crucial importance of intention to the appliance of action. Light and dark motives, white and black magic, good and bad outcomes.

Mystics through the ages have generally used their knowledge and skills to boost the positive vibration. Malicious practitioners have done the opposite.

There are mystical expressions of all the major religions – Islam, Judaism, Christianity, Hinduism, Buddhism, Confucianism Wicca, Druidry and the rest.

All incorporate the ancient wisdom of alchemy, astrology, numerology and the uses of sound, colour, the human chakras, the Earth's energy lines, visions, vibrations, symbols and other such pathways to enlightenment.

I suppose brought up as a Christian, it's the mystical aspects of that faith that attract me the most. But I'm more of a Theosophist, seeing eternal truth in all belief systems.

Above all, I'm a free thinker, searching for truth wherever it can be found. Restrictive labels repel and annoy me.

I'm fascinated on finding connections and similarities between the stories and sayings of the various faiths, dating way back to ancient Egypt, Sumeria and Mesopotamia.

Yes it's true – All we know and have in our modern civilisations originated in those Middle Eastern lands currently being torn apart by war and civil unrest.

They remain the battle grounds of conflicting ideas and those passionate to spread them. And there are a lot of natural resources there to be plundered and annexed.

****

CHAPTER SIX – ALTERNATIVE HISTORIES

April 23 – Happy St George's Day! It's also the 400th anniversary of Shakespeare's death. US President Barak Obama, on a visit to England, is among those marking the occasion – by visiting a London theatre dedicated to the playwright's work.

Any lyric writer worth his salt looks up to Shakespeare, Dylan Thomas, Lewis Carroll and the great poets. I certainly do.

April 24 – Went to the Bell last night and had a great time listening to tribute band Total Madness and chatting to Mark and Laura, John Gaynor, Nicola Williams, her mum Penny and others.

It was the first lengthy conversation I'd had with Penny, a nice lady with a sweet nature. I can see where Nicola gets it from.

From mates to music… Jake Bugg and Keith Richards both dig the Everly Brothers. So do Paul McCartney, Paul Simon and a host of other artists. How cool is that?

Oh, and Prince, Bowie, Lemmy, Glen Frey's Eagles and Maurice White's Earth, Wind and Fire have all influenced many groups and singers.

Prince, in turn, was inspired by Roxy Music and Gary Numan, Bowie by John Coltrane and the Velvet Underground, Frey by Elvis Presley and Neil Young, EWF by Jimi Hendrix and Marvin Gaye while Lemmy was a massive Beatles fan.

Quality music rules okay?

Speaking of which, yesterday I listened to a bit of Tom Petty and today I've been playing McCartney's superb album Venus and Mars. It's time for my Sunday dinner now so I'm going to slap on the brilliant Who's Next while I cook it.

April 25 – Been playing the quite wonderful White Album this morning. Can't beat a bit of Beatles!

We are all sparks of consciousness – awareness – wrapped in physical bodies to experience a five-sense world while striving towards a greater understanding of the spiritual realms. But far too many folk acquiesce to the mundane, ignoring the divine.

And even those who see beyond and acknowledge the callous manipulation of the five-sense reality by the unscrupulous often draw the wrong conclusions. No doubt I do all the time. But life is a learning curve, so they say. Or at least it should be.

I've noticed that a lot of the conspiracy theorists banging on about the Illuminati and the New World Order are right-wing Christian nuts obsessed with the notion that all politicians, captains of industry and showbiz celebrities are Satanists or their puppets.

Yes, I'm sure there's a ruthless, vicious elite in charge wanting to grab all the power and wealth. Their motives are very dark and they use divide and rule to keep control.

Are we moving with accelerating speed towards a future governed by a global fascist state? Almost certainly, I'd say. But it will become less and less likely as more and more people wake up, see through the smokescreen and challenge the game plan.

But whether the obnoxious manipulators are all Satanists or members of the Illuminati, who can tell? – Unless they have personal experience of course.

April 26 – Phew! Time to breathe a sigh of relief. Just got back from seeing Dr Mitchell to discuss the results of my recent blood test and 24-hour BP monitoring.

He said my liver, kidneys and blood/sugar levels were fine but my cholesterol reading was still above normal although it had inexplicably fallen very slightly from last year.

Once again he offered me the chance to take cholesterol-reducing pills in addition to my normal daily beta-blocker and soluble

Aspirin. But he didn't insist on it, left it up to me and seemed happy enough when I declined.

I remain at greater risk of stroke or heart attack than most men of my age, but this is also fractionally reduced from last year's estimation, probably due to the cholesterol result.

So it's see you again this time or thereabouts in 2017, barring any other unexpected reasons arising to consult him before then. Excellent!

My continued studies of alternative histories and belief systems has led me to a documentary about the Sumerians that I watched on You Tube last night. Fascinating!

The Sumerian culture, dating back 8,000 years, is the oldest one known on Earth. These people knew astrology, astronomy, farming and medicine and we still use the same mathematical system and calendar that they established all those millennia ago.

Various intriguing texts and paintings have been discovered that are said to tell their story, leading to the amazing assertion that humanity's origins lie in the stars.

It's claimed that a race called the Annunaki arrived here is spaceships to genetically engineer the resident species, Homo erectus. The result was Homo sapiens – us – a slave race to serve these invaders regarded as gods.

Some even declare that descendants of these invaders are still with us – the elite bloodlines.

This ties in with Bible mentioning the Nephilim, a pre-Flood race described as the sons of God who had children with the daughters of men.

Incidentally, the Genesis account of Noah's Flood is remarkably similar to a tale told in Sumerian texts dating back considerably further. So are the Garden of Eden and several other very well-known Bible stories.

Oh, and Jewish mythology mentions Adam's first wife, Lilith, created at the same time as him.

Eve, of course, was made later. The Bible tells us this was from one of Adam's ribs, but it's now thought rib here is a mistranslation of a similar Hebrew word meaning breath – which makes a lot more sense actually.

As I write, I'm savouring the sonic delights of the Icicle Works, the 1984 debut album by the Liverpool group of the same name. Terrific!

A bit earlier I played A Young Person's Guide to King Crimson. I don't like everything Robert Fripp and company did, but there's some mighty fine tracks here and I love this compilation album.

Remember what I said about the shiver up and down the spine that all the best music gives me? The Night Watch and Starless do it to me every time.

April 26, 9pm – Had a lovely few hours at the Bell with Mark, Laura, Nicola and Dave. It snowed while I was there. Yes, snowed! (Last April I attended a barbeque).

On the way home from the pub, a bit wobbly, I tripped on an uneven part of the pavement and fell over. Several total strangers came to my rescue to check on me.

When all's said and done, things happen every day to restore your faith in human nature. And that's cool. But I did incur a few tender cuts and bruises.

April 27 – At last! Justice for the 96 football fans who died in the 1989 Hillsborough disaster. An inquest jury decided yesterday that they were unlawfully killed.

The decision vindicated the Liverpool supporters who had previously been held responsible for the fatal crush that also injured 766 at an FA Cup semi-final against Nottingham Forest staged at Sheffield Wednesday's home ground.

Jurors found that police failures before and during the match led to the tragedy.

There are calls for top officers to be prosecuted as two criminal investigations rumble on that could finish by the end of 2016.

Families and friends have been seething for 27 years at what they consider police incompetence and a cynical attempt to cover up what happened and blame the fans.

The Sun newspaper remains extremely unpopular and widely boycotted in Liverpool after it criticized the crowd in a scathing attack a few days after the disaster.

April 28 – Families of the crush victims have welcomed the suspension of South Yorkshire's top cop, Chief Constable David Crompton, in the wake of the inquest findings. But this raises an obvious question – was he involved at Hillsborough?

It was 27 years ago. What was his rank then? Was he even in the force? And, most importantly, was he at the football ground on that fateful day?

If so, then his suspension is fully warranted. But if not, this smacks to me of a token gesture many moons after the fact making him a scapegoat while the real offenders get off scot free.

Some would argue that Crompton's spearheading of attempts to fabricate inquest evidence and pin blame for the disaster wholly on the football fans was reason enough. A fair point.

Plus the fact that he's been outspokenly critical of the Liverpool supporters' behaviour at Hillsborough.

And he and his officers have been in hot water more than once in the recent past.

His force came under fire for failing to tackle organised child abuse in Rotherham.

There are calls for a public inquiry into officers' conduct in the so-called Battle of Orgreave police-picket confrontation during the 1984-5 miners' strike.

And Crompton came under personal verbal attack over his officers' involvement in a botched and ultimately embarrassing raid on Sir Cliff Richard's Berkshire home in 2014 following an allegation of child abuse.

Sir Cliff hotly denied the claim, no evidence was found, no charges brought and no further action taken.

So maybe the chief constable's suspension and the dissolution of South Yorkshire police force are long overdue. Or possibly its radical reform. At the very least probing questions should be asked over its conduct in all these cases.

But I still have a horrible feeling that no further action will be taken, those directly responsible for the Hillsborough cock ups and cover up will escape prosecution and all these controversies will be once again be swept under the carpet.

April 29 – The Labour Party is currently embroiled in a row over alleged "anti-Semitic" remarks – just as we prepare to go to the voting booths next Thursday. A coincidence? I think not!

The furore has erupted over Facebook comments made two years ago by Bradford West MP Naz Shah.

She was critical of Israel and suggested flippantly that relocating that territory and its inhabitants to within USA borders would solve a lot of problems in the Middle East.

This has been taken by some as an attack on Jewish people in general and she's been suspended as a fierce debate rages on.

Defending her, Fellow Labourite Ken Livingstone, former Mayor of London, said her unfortunate remark about Israel was certainly not intended as a slur on all Jews.

He was absolutely right and I fully supported him up to that point. But, badgered to

elaborate, he then made his own ill-advised remark about Adolf Hitler which only made matters far worse, leading party leader Jeremy Corbin to suspend him as well.

Naz Shah has now apologized for her rather silly and clumsy comments. I find the current timing of the heated dispute over those two-year-old remarks so interesting.

For starters, it's all pretty embarrassing for Sadiq Khan, Labour's candidate for the London Mayoral elections – also next Thursday. He had been the front-runner.

Another coincidence? Yeah right! Politics is such a vicious, dishonourable business.

With police commissioner and some local council polls being held the same day, the constant recurrence of by-elections and Labour enjoying a rush of new members and revived popularity with the masses, it seems some have decided to play real dirty.

It's so easy to blacken anyone's name by misrepresenting the facts, quoting out of context and wildly exaggerating the importance and intention of what's been said.

I have myself in the past asserted that criticizing the political agenda of Israel's Zionist leaders is certainly not an attack on Jews in general or Semites in particular.

And I've warned of the dire dangers of confusing the three. Zionism is a political ideology, Judaism a religion and Semitic a very specific term for people and cultures traditionally speaking the Semitic language.

According to Wikipedia, the racial use of the description, together with its parallels Hamitic and Japhetic, is now obsolete. (Shem, Ham and Japheth were sons of Noah.)

It adds that, according to some scholars, the concept of Semitic ethnicity doesn't exist so the term should actually be avoided.

I maintain that to suggest that anti-Semite, anti-Zionist and anti-Jewish are the same thing is deliberately misleading – with possibly disastrous consequences.

Under extreme pressure, Corbin has had little choice but suspend both Shah and Livingstone in order to distance himself and his party from the raging controversy.

But all three have insisted that bigoted and racist remarks have no place in Labour's ranks, Livingstone and Khan adding adamantly that they never meant for their comments to be taken that way.

I just think it's all a massive storm in a teacup, whipped up to ridiculous proportions by mischief makers in a cynical attempt to discredit a resurgent Labour party.

Racism doesn't come into it. It's politics, pure and simple. And the worst kind – savage and underhand.

Anyone who knows me will appreciate that I'm coming from the position of someone who finds racism and bigotry of all descriptions ignorant, despicable and nonsensical.

But I do reserve the right to disagree with and criticize others' political views and actions without resorting to petty, nasty attacks on them or their peers of any kind.

If I've ever appeared to, it would have been while lambasting people for disgraceful behaviour, not slating them for what they were. I've been angry, scathing and bitterly sarcastic but never personal. At least I've not meant it to be interpreted as such.

Mentioning Israel once again takes me back to the Middle East and those cradle of civilisation lands and their comparative texts.

The Sumerians believed in a pantheon of gods and goddesses but their chief deity – often equated with the Christian God, Jewish Yahweh and Muslim Allah – was Anu, God of Heaven.

He had two sons by different mothers – and those sons were Enki and Enlil.

According to the texts, they were aliens who came to Earth to mine for gold. But then they genetically engineered a slave race using the resident population and put them to work doing the hard labour.

These slaves, our North African ancestors, were made less intelligent, more docile and obedient and, most importantly, cut off from higher truths and their higher selves.

Enlil became the Lord of this World – and still is thanks to his cruel, self-centred and avaricious descendents bred in his image. I would add driven by the negative current.

Meanwhile, the (some claim) far nicer, caring Enki constantly strives to win back power (for all our sakes) working through divinely inspired, enlightened teachers. In my parlance, carriers of the positive vibration of love and peace.

Much of this appears to be backed up by the Book of Enoch, one of the Dead Sea Scrolls. Enoch, said to be Noah's great grandfather, is briefly mentioned in the Bible.

He speaks of the Annunaki coming from a planet called Nibiru. He also seems to support the Nephilim theory; referring to a mysterious race he calls the Watchers.

And a lot of the Sumerian texts and alternative ancient documents found at Qumran and Nag Hammadi seem to overlap and complement familiar Biblical accounts.

Talking of overlaps, it's intriguing to note that Y'Shua (Jesus) apparently wasn't the first famous man in history reputed to be have been born of a virgin. It's alleged he had at least two predecessors.

The Egyptian mother goddess Isis, wife of Osiris, is said to have been intact on producing their son Horus – interestingly enough, on December 25.

And the Babylonian shepherd god Tammuz was described as being conceived by a sunbeam. His mother was Nimrod's wife Semiramis, known to some as the Statue of Liberty at the entrance to New York Harbour.

I'd suggest that all three virgin birth accounts are in truth deep symbolism, not to be taken too literally.

I always thought that such claims were a biological nonsense anyway. But I've just Googled it and found out – to my astonishment – that in fact it IS possible for a woman who's not had full-on sex, or with hymen still intact, to have a baby.

Granted it's very rare, but there have been recorded cases throughout history and they continue to be occasionally made – and widely disbelieved.

Apparently, the advent of IVF technology – helping infertile women have their own children – has made it more likely.

So all three holy men might have been born of virgins after all. But I still tend to think that in their cases, the assertion is meant to convey the fact that they were considered to be very special, extremely advanced spiritually and imbued with great divinity.

Christianity's central character is often compared to these two earlier religious icons thanks to the striking similarities in descriptions of their qualities and achievements.

And although we celebrate Christmas on December 25, some say it was chosen to coincide with and replace existing festivals marking the claimed birth dates of various pagan gods either on that day or about the time of the winter solstice (December 21).

Revised dates for Y'shua bar Yosef (Jesus son of Joseph) put his birth at April 17 in the year 6 BC (BCE to non-Christians) and his crucifixion on Friday April 7, AD 30.

Making another swift subject change, I'd like to wish Sam and Carl's son Bailey a happy fourth birthday.

Oh, and for those even remotely interested, Kings of Leon, Foo Fighters, the Verve and Peter Green's Fleetwood Mac.

April 30 – Sticking with music, there was a good two-hour documentary on BBC Four telly yesterday evening about the Dave Clark Five.

They're not mentioned much these days but for four years back in the 1960s they were huge.

This side of the Atlantic, they were seen as serious rivals to the Beatles and the Stones. And in the USA they had more success than any other band except Lennon's.

Sir Paul McCartney, Sir Cliff Richard, Ozzy Osbourne, Stevie Wonder, Bruce Springsteen, Elton John, Freddie Mercury, Dionne Warwick and Gene Simmons all sang the praises of drummer and songwriter Dave and his group.

The band split up in 1970 but Clark – who had also been its manager and producer – went on to set up his own media company and bought the rights to the iconic sixties TV show Ready Steady Go!, which all the big chart acts of those days appeared on.

He also wrote and produced the highly-acclaimed London stage musical Time, narrated by Sir Laurence Olivier. It was seen by more than a million people.

A two-disc vinyl album was released in conjunction with the stage production, featuring music performed by Sir Cliff, Julian Lennon, Freddie Mercury and Stevie Wonder. The album and its accompanying singles sold over 12 million copies.

Oh bum! – Writing about Olivier just then has spurred me to check on something and realize I've blundered in a massive way.

I unforgivably left Sir Laurence – the greatest actor in my lifetime – out of my list of favourites in Volume Seven, Persistent Illusions. What a silly Billy I am! Sorry pal!

It's as bad as omitting Bob Dylan from my rundown of favourite male rock stars.

I've enjoyed CDs by Humble Pie, Steel Pulse and Gary Numan in the last two days.

But yesterday (Saturday) I also had a whale of a time in pleasant weather at the Bell's family fun day in aid of the ex-services personnel's charity Homes for Heroes.

I chatted to loads of mates as I spent a few hours there in the afternoon and then went back for a shorter while in the evening.

Steam engines, a big bouncy castle, stalls and a barbeque were among the attractions and my friend John Palmer was deejay.

Guv'nors Laura Williams and Mark Evans thoroughly relished being in charge of proceedings along with bar manager Nicola Williams and barman, co-organiser and engine driver for the day Dave Froud, ably assisted by their super team.

Nicola's feller Mark, Jem and Tony Hannen, Simon "Squeak" Turnbull, his lady Ruth, Dawn Lewis, Mark "Tich" Hemington, Matt Brant, Ben Avill, Candice Clayton, Nicola's mum Penny, Ollie Okoye, Billy Clarkson and my pals Jim, Ian, Brian and Darren (don't know their surnames) were also in attendance.

Music for the evening was provided by the very good 1960s covers band Prairie Dogs. I hadn't seen them before and was impressed.

Oh, and my very close friend of the past two decades or so, Paula Carruthers – she of the six-month relationship mentioned in Volume 11 and earlier in this one – turned up with her new man Mark Flint to have beers and burgers in the afternoon.

I had actually invited Paula a few weeks ago, when she said she was missing seeing her chums from Pokesdown and the pub, but she'd reminded me that she usually works Saturdays so probably wouldn't be able to make it.

So imagine my surprise when I saw her and Mark walk in. Paula explained that her doctor had signed her off from work for two weeks as she was suffering from stress.

About time too! – It finally gives her a chance to recuperate and regain her strength after putting up with undue pressure and demands at Ferndown's Tesco store for ages.

Mark had accompanied her because, although he works many weekends, he also had the day off.

Getting home from the pub, I watched a TV programme comprising old footage of the late great American comedian Bill Hicks in concert.

This very funny guy pulled no punches in lampooning modern society's attitudes in a satirical, sarcastic and seriously searing way. But he was also extremely perceptive.

He knew the score all right and he came out with some amazingly profound wisdom alongside many hilarious comments reflecting his refreshingly truthful take on life.

This is one of my favourite quotes of his. I've used it before in a previous book, but it's so brilliant it's worth repeating here:

"All matter is merely energy condensed to a slow vibration. We are all one consciousness experiencing itself subjectively. There is no such thing as death, life is only a dream and we are the imagination of ourselves."

Wow! – How damned good is that? Spot on Bill, you've nailed it mate.

May 1 – Happy birthday Becca, Sam Excell's daughter.

May 2 – It's a bank holiday Monday today. Yesterday evening I had another great session at the Bell with Mark "Tich" Hemington, Penny Williams, Louise Delahaye, John Gaynor, Jeff McNally, Matt Brant, deejay Ross Maslin and others.

It all got a bit messy when someone had the bright idea of doing shots.

Lou in particular was being flirty, extremely suggestive and quite outrageous, to the chagrin of her son Michael – Mikey – a barman at the pub but off duty at the time.

Penny, of course, is bar manager Nicola's mum. Nic was working last night.

As I said to Lou, you realize you've still got it when you can still embarrass your offspring. Ha ha!

You know something? I'm once again experiencing a feel good factor after the heartbreak and trauma I went through not all that long ago.

I'm hopeful, more alive than I have been for a while and I no longer see myself residing in others' shadows, which I did for far too bloody long. It's liberating!

I can once again, at long last, be me and express myself. I've started wearing hats.

I'm playing a Yes compilation album as I write. Excellent! – Another band that can produce that spinal shiver. Their classic long player Close to the Edge is number 11 in my top 50 all-time favourites.

Yesterday I listened to the good debut album by so-called super group Asia, featuring Yes lead guitarist Steve Howe alongside ace drummer Carl Palmer of ELP.

May 3 – Leicester City have won the English Premier League in one of football's most unlikely fairytale endings.

The 5,000 to one outsiders at the start of the season are guaranteed to lift the top flight's prestigious trophy after nearest rivals Tottenham Hotspurs could only manage a draw against Chelsea yesterday evening.

The victorious team will presented with the silverware in front of thousands of delighted fans at their home match against Everton on Saturday.

There's also very good news for AFC Bournemouth of course. With just two matches left to play, they're sure of remaining in the Premier League for at least another season after winning promotion to it for the first time ever last May.

Right lads – next year top half of the table, the one after that, Champions' League, eh? Hey, we can all dream! And with their superb manager Eddie Howe in charge, who knows?

I'm not alone in seeing Eddie as a future strong contender for the England job. But we Cherries fans obviously want him to stay put at the Vitality Stadium, Dean Court, for as long as possible.

May 4 – Sun shining brightly in a sapphire blue, largely cloudless sky, sea a gorgeous deeper shade of blue, grass lush green and carrying that lovely freshly-cut smell, strikingly beautiful vistas of Bournemouth Bay.

This was the scene at 9.30am today as I sat on a cliff top bench taking in the splendour. I thought to myself – fantastic, it doesn't get much better than this!

I find it so very sad that thousands of people who live in my beloved seaside town either don't get the chance to enjoy this fundamental, profound, healthy, wonderfully therapeutic and totally free experience on their doorsteps or simply can't be bothered.

It also makes me acutely aware of the troubles and strife being suffered by all those who aren't as lucky as me. Victims of tragedy, war, terrorism, terrible accidents and terminal illness.

My own cousin Sandra continues her grim battle against cancer. It was her birthday yesterday and, by pure chance, I saw her man Alan in Boots the Chemists' Southbourne branch. He agreed to give her my love and wish her well for me.

(I'd popped a card in the post to her last week with a similar message.)

I'm now listening to The Housemartins. Earlier, it was The The. Yesterday it was Cat Stevens and the Beat.

May 5 – Just been to vote for our local police commissioner. Other parts of the country are holding council elections and Londoners are choosing their next Mayor.

It will be very interesting to see in the next couple of days how that ridiculous Labour Party bust up over so-called anti-Semitism has affected these polls.

I say so-called for the reasons explained earlier. You can oppose Zionism – as Naz Shah clearly does – without criticising Jews or Semites.

As I've said, these terms have three distinctly different meanings and to confuse them, deliberately or not, can lead to all sorts of problems – as we've seen in this case.

I abhor some of the vicious tactics of Zionists in Israel, terrorising and killing Palestinians who actually have a greater claim to that land than they do.

But I also detest the savage and lethal actions of some of those on the other side. Or any side – Muslim, Jewish, Christian, whatever. They're all violent nut jobs.

I actually feel so sorry for the millions of honest, decent, genuine Jews (and Muslims and Christians) caught up in and callously exploited in this insanity that has its roots in the Holocaust, the politics of the State of Israel and far older ideological clashes.

Some folk have outrageously denied the Holocaust took place, or at least tried to play down the mass murder and misery involved. Others have over-exaggerated its scale and impacts.

How the Hell can anyone, Jewish or not, pick out the truth from the lies in this deeply divisive, destructive and apparently endless propaganda conflict?

Israel was set up after World War Two to give followers of Judaism their own homeland in accordance with a long-held ideal expressed in both the Torah and Bible.

The huge problem here was that it was established by brute force in a territory long occupied and surrounded by those of the Muslim religion – Islam.

This meant displacing people traditionally linked for ages to that land by blood and soil to make way for a fresh influx of foreign newcomers who just happened to be of the Jewish faith. Only some living in the areas mentioned in the Holy texts are or ever have been.

Hence the Arab-Israeli wars and the ongoing Palestinian crisis.

The formation of Israel further aggravated centuries-old cultural battles between Judaism, Islam and Christianity in the Holy Land – holy to all three religions that is.

One of the many outcomes of this was that the words Zionist, Jewish and Semite became inextricably mixed up – a confusion ruthlessly exploited by some for purely political reasons that have little or nothing to do with either faith or race.

The admittedly tactless Naz Shah and Ken Livingstone recently became embroiled in this crazy, totally unnecessary propaganda war as it was escalated to absurd levels.

I say there are far too many cases of offensive and misleading words being recklessly bandied about. And a whole heap of needless resentment and strife in the world.

As a peace-loving pacifist, I frequently despair at the intolerance and brutality of others – regardless of race, religion, cultural preferences or political views.

Come on guys – live and let live eh? If someone says something that upsets you, ignore them. Don't make mountains out of molehills. Be the bigger person.

I'm now playing the iconic and influential Shadows as I type. A bit earlier I listened to the excellent Iron Maiden, who I've seen three times live.

The first occasion was at Bournemouth Winter Gardens on their Killers tour when Paul Di'Anno was still lead vocalist.

Bruce Dickinson had taken over the role by the second time I saw them at Poole Arts Centre on the Number of the Beast tour. The third gig by them I attended was at the same venue when they were promoting the Powerslave album.

They blew me away all three times and they're one of my favourite hard rock bands. They're number 20 in my run-down of my favourite groups of all time.

If you don't think that's very impressive, you need to check out the list. It's in Volume Seven, Persistent Illusions. Making the top 50 is no mean feat!

May 6 – Labour did better than expected in the yesterday's local council elections, picking up more seats than anticipated.

So, thank heavens, the "anti-Semite" dirty tricks campaign didn't work, failing to have the adverse impact its instigators had intended. Good – I hope it means people saw through the spiteful, unwarranted bull crap.

Although not a big fan of Labour (I'm a card-carrying Green), I think it would have been bad for the country if the attempt to slur a resurgent red brigade had borne fruit.

Why? Because it would have further degraded politics, already far too often a filthy underhand business, and undermined the whole concepts of democracy and fairness.

At least under Jeremy Corbyn Labour resembles a proper socialist alternative once again after the irritating Blair/Brown wannabe Tory years when you couldn't see the difference between the two main parties. It's also closer to Green ideals than it was.

Last night I watched a shocking two-hour TV film called *Hillsborough*, a dramatized account of the disaster that's recently been in the news again.

Christopher Eccleston and Ricky Tomlinson both gave powerful performances as grieving fathers angered and disgusted by the subsequent lies and cover-up attempt.

I found the film on Catch Up TV. I was having great fun in the pub on Sunday night when it was actually broadcast.

The movie graphically showed that police incompetence, not rowdy drunken fans, caused the tragedy that killed 96 Liverpool supporters at that fateful FA Cup tie.

And it went on to pull no punches in detailing the cynical cover up attempt that followed as the Sun newspaper printed outrageous and totally unfounded allegations that laid the blame squarely at the crowd's feet.

I appreciated more fully than ever the deep resentment and bitter fury of the victims' families at the cold and calculated diversion tactics as officers tried to avoid prosecution.

Okay, fair enough, it's easy to be wise after the event and just maybe some of the fans' enthusiasm got the better of them. But it seems that officers' dreadful handling of the situation turned a crisis that could have been minimised into a terrible tragedy.

And the lies and blame-shifting that followed were unforgivable. Those responsible for this post-match disgrace should be held to account – both police and Press. Incensed families are understandably demanding prison sentences for the culprits.

While prattling on here, I'm playing the awesome Led Zeppelin double album the Song Remains the Same, containing live performances also featured in the film of the same name, centred on a legendary show at Madison Square Garden, New York, in

Reviewing this masterpiece when it was released, a music journalist for the *Melody Maker* – or was it the *New Musical Express*? I can't remember which – said that sides two and three of the vinyl long player proved the group's true musical genius.

I totally agree. Those two vinyl sides had No Quarter, Stairway to Heaven and a 27-minute version of Dazed and Confused. It's one of the most stunning aural sensations I've ever had.

Speaking as someone who's regrettably never seen Zeppelin live, I think listening to the album or, better still, watching the movie is the next best thing. You really get a terrific idea of what this incredible band was all about.

I'm listening to a 2007 reissue of the album on CD with six extra tracks, but bought that original vinyl double LP when it first came out in 1975.

I also saw the accompanying mind-blowing film – the first movie shown at Reading's ABC cinema after it installed a quadraphonic sound system. All I can say is – wow!

That's why Led Zeppelin remain my second favourite band ever after the Beatles.

You know I said earlier in this book that people are in our lives for a reason but not necessarily the one we think? I can see with the benefit of hindsight that Paula is an excellent example of this.

Before her return I'd long given up on the idea of ever having a man-woman relationship with anyone beyond being close, loving but platonic pals. Even before my confidence-shattering heart crisis, I had felt that door was closed to me. Besides, I was permanently skint so it wasn't an option.

As time went on, I got so accustomed to being on my own (well, in that sense at least – treasured family and close friends notwithstanding) that I'd settled for it and was quite content to do so.

I've frequently said, with more determination than enthusiasm, that I'm perfectly happy and have the luxury of doing what I want when I want without consulting anyone else. I got stuck in a rut and didn't mind one bit – or so I told myself.

But Paula changed all that – and she was the perfect person to do so.

Before last summer, I wouldn't have had the nerve to try and strike up new friendships with women that might or might not lead to a sexual partnership.

The fact that we'd been friends for 20 years, had already shared intimacy and were both comfortable, therefore relaxed with each other was the key to my restoration. I could never have been that brave or forward with someone I was just getting to know.

I was gutted when it finished, just as I was daring to think long-term. Apparently it wasn't meant to be. But now I see a lot more clearly that Paula's actually done me a massive favour.

I can now, at long last, think in terms of having a female life partner. And I have the confidence to look for one among the women I see and chat to.

Paula's made me realize, to my great joy and relief, that there's still life in this old dog yet. I feel like a teenager again – revived. Thanks Paula. Thanks an awful lot, girl!

And I've retained her as a long-term, close mate who loves me as much as I love her. Again, that probably wouldn't have happened had we not been the best of pals to start with.

I'm well aware that what I'm now saying contradicts the prose and lyrics I wrote at the time of the deeply painful split with Paula that coincided with our very good friend Theresa's passing.

But there again, a lot of what I've said in recent times has been different to opinions expressed in my earlier books.

I stand by all I've written because in every case it was a true reflection of how I was feeling at that particular time. We can all change our minds as life goes on, new experiences unfold and extra facts come to light.

So I'm dressing different, saying different things and acting differently. So what! Tomorrow, or next week, month or year I might be changing again.

It's called living a life and learning from it. And it's all part of the vibrant joy of existence.

Because I'm writing an ongoing contemporaneous journal about current events, experiences and my thoughts on them, there's always a time lapse between my actually typing my words on a computer screen and their appearing in published form.

Things can change, quite dramatically sometimes, during that interim period, and when I get the final proofs before my books go to print there's always the chance – and temptation – to amend my words in light of new facts and altered circumstances.

But I refuse to do this because it would invalidate the topicality of my ramblings. To tamper after the fact would mean my comments were no longer a true reflection of how I was feeling when I wrote them.

The most obvious example of this in my personal life of late has been what I call the Paula situation. Our reunion and subsequent short relationship changed my circumstances and feelings dramatically – twice over.

As always, I was writing about what I was feeling at the time – in my last book *Amazing Messages* and earlier in this one. I was, of course, blissfully unaware of how things would turn out so very differently from how I at that point envisaged.

I could now easily change what I said at the start of this volume before submitting it to my publishers. I could even amend what I wrote in the last one when I get the final proofs before it goes to print. But I won't.

I hope Paula doesn't mind. We're such close friends I don't think she will. It would be a simple matter to meddle with my writings but I don't see why I should.

Granted, I do revise my song lyrics, sometimes years afterwards. But I won't mess around with my prose journal entries giving my concurrent take on the truth as I see it at any particular time. That would discredit the whole enterprise.

I can also change my opinions as news stories unfold and I gain more wisdom through books, TV shows and documentaries. My views now might be different from what they were previously, expressed in earlier books.

May 7 – Labour's Sadiq Khan is London's new mayor, replacing eccentric Tory Boris Johnson.

Khan's victory over his Conservative Party rival Zac Goldsmith was further proof that the ridiculous "anti-Semite" smear campaign hadn't worked.

Labour also did well in the Welsh Assembly poll the same day, securing 29 of the 60 seats. UKIP picking up seven stopped the reds having an overall majority.

Plaid Cymru's 12 seats included a notable triumph for party leader Leanne Wood, who beat Labour's Leighton Andrews in Rhondda.

Tory defector Neil Hamilton was among UKIP's successful seven. The Conservatives ended up with 11 seats and the Liberal Democrats, just one.

But north of the border, in Scotland, Labour lost ground as the Conservatives increased their share of the seats from 15 to 31. Labour secured 24 against last time's 37. The SNP lost six seats but remains the biggest party with 63.

The Lib Dems picked up five, same as last time, but slipped to fifth place behind the Greens, who trebled their tally from two seats to six. I find this very encouraging.

We didn't have any local council or Parliamentary elections in Bournemouth but we were asked to choose our police commissioner.

With no Green candidate standing, I voted for Independent Martyn Underhill to retain the post which he did. He promises to keep politics out of policing – not a bad thing in my view.

I'm currently playing The Best of New Order on my stereo system. Very good it is too. Earlier I was listening to a Bee Gees compilation taking in all their hits from the sixties pop rock classics to the disco anthems. Cool!

I saw two excellent documentary films on You Tube back to back last night called *Zeitgeist* and *Zeitgeist Addendum*. There's a third, *Zeitgeist the Way Forward*, which I haven't seen yet but will do later today.

I've heard the word zeitgeist many times but not known until now what it meant. These movies, that I would thoroughly recommend, explain in an intriguing, thought-provoking way. I guess a rough sum-up of the term could be "spirit of the age."

And a lot of the contents and assertions of these two-hour documentaries fit in perfectly with what I've been thinking and saying for the past few years. I'm looking forward to seeing the third, most recently made instalment later.

May 10 – The third Zeitgeist documentary was as good as the first two.

The guy responsible, Peter Joseph, is an American independent film maker who was a professional musician and equity trader before having a bit of an epiphany and going into the alternative media.

Zeitgeist, which has now become a movement, asserts that all the major religions have the same basic source, which is why they tell the same stories but with different names and locations.

And that shared source is firmly rooted in ancient astrological and solar belief systems. Spot on!

Zeitgeist people also propose a radical alternative system of government based on a resource-based economy, not money.

This means that rather than plundering the natural environment in a crass, thoughtless drive based on cash, profit and blinkered selfish greed, we should respect that there are limits to our exploitation of resources and make flora, fauna and people the central feature – not the opposite that we have now.

And we should realize that there are unlimited alternative energy sources that could be supplied free of charge with a minimum impact on our environment in preference to the illogical reliance on very finite and fast depleting fossil fuels whose days are numbered.

Of course, the big problem here is that a lot of amazingly powerful people have very lucrative vested interests in maintaining the outdated, seriously polluting oil-based system we so totally rely on.

And they're all too eager to invade countries with those dollar and pound generating resources – and all on the feeble unsubstantiated pretext of staving off terrorism threatening the West. Yeah, right!

More and more people are seeing through this bull shit and waking up to the truth. I was a late arrival on the bus but now I urge you all to climb aboard. Don't tolerate exploitation, unfairness or hatred.

Sod the obsessive bread heads and their political lackeys. They've had their day. It's our turn now. The quiet and peaceful revolution is underway. Power to the people – right on!

In this respect I'm very much with Peter Joseph, David Icke, Russell Brand and the late great wise men Bill Hicks, John Lennon, George Harrison and Bob Marley; Einstein, Carl Jung and Plato. And of course the daddy of them all – the transcendent Mahatma Gandhi. Now what a guy he was.

Russell Brand? Well yes. I know a lot of people don't like him, calling him a fake and a self-righteous, grating big head. But he has a skilled way with words and I find him very funny. I believe his heart's in the right place, his ideas are sound and he's on our side against a corrupt system.

May 10, 9pm – Today I've been at the Bell with Paula. We're okay. Anyone who sides with either of us over our unfortunate but maybe inevitable split is kinda missing the point. We love each other very much – have done for years, always will do – and we've each done the other a massive favour.

I gave her that last, crucial little piece of confidence she desperately needed to get out of a situation that was becoming intolerable for her. She, in turn, made me realize I was still capable of having a romantic, sexual man-woman relationship.

We've both gained a lot from our largely happy reunion –even though there's been pain and tears along the way for us both.

She's found another partner. I live in hope. And thanks to her, I feel confident enough to believe it's possible for me too. I hope to fall in love again and if I do I'll give it my all. It will be for keeps. Thanks Paula!

Yeah, as I said, people are in your life for a reason – but not always the one you think. It's often only in retrospect that you appreciate this.

May 11 – Yesterday's rendezvous with Paula in my beloved Bell was our monthly drinks and catch-up session. We chatted to Mark and Laura, barmaid Demi (I do hope I'm spelling her name right), barmen Dave and Mikey and regulars Matt, Ian, Lee, Darren and Brian.

Today is the anniversary of reggae star Bob Marley's death in 1981. That guy was brilliant, a true musical icon and an admirable wise man spreading a message of hope, love and peace. Excellent!

It's also the anniversary of the Bradford City football stadium fire in 1985, in which 56 died and more than 260 injured.

I've lit a candle for Bob and the Bradford 56 and I'm playing a bit of Marley as I write.

I had Ocean Colour Scene on the stereo the other day. Variety is the spice of life, eh?

May 12 – I'm just playing a live album by Johnny Cash. Man, that guy was one of the coolest dudes on the planet! He could also write good songs and perform them well alongside great versions of other people's work.

He was no angel but I get the feeling he had a good heart. Anyone who can lay down pure, authentic emotion-charged tracks like that just has to have.

I'm currently reading Dan Brown's book *Inferno*. Like all his others, it's really thought-provoking.

Once again it's a fast-paced thriller built around a race against time to stave off a global disaster. And once again the central character is Robert Langdon, the American symbologist played by Tom Hanks in the films *Angels and Demons* and the *Da Vinci Code*, both based on earlier Brown books.

This time the impending apocalyptic crisis is the unleashing of a worldwide plague intended to dramatically cull a fast-growing population before it outstrips resources leading to deprivation, starvation, chaos and billions of deaths of its own.

The book's villain claims that the ideal number of people on the planet would be four billion but we're already at seven billion and it's fast spiralling out of control.

It's alarming to realize there's at least some truth in this. It's a fact that the current global population is calculated at 7.125 billion and it's expected to reach 8.4 billion by 2030.

It's also a sobering thought that this growth is exponential. In the year 1000 it was 400 million, by 1927 it had risen to two billion, by 1960 it was three billion and by 2000 it was six billion. Now it's over seven billion and if it carries on multiplying at the same rate in will double again more quickly.

Life expectancy has steadily increased as cures are found for ailments and we haven't had a big epidemic for centuries or a world war since the 1940s to kill off millions as they used to.

Rather than exterminating all over-60s, starting a new global conflict or releasing a mass-murdering chemical or biological virus, it's apparently a matter of paramount importance that less drastic solutions are found to this growing problem. But what?

Well, birth control is one obvious answer – but this raises all sorts of awkward questions as to how it would be implemented.

Some conspiracy theorists assert that the dark elite running the show is poised to dramatically cull the world population one way or another – possibly starting this year.

Others suspect a cure for cancer has already been found but its being kept from the general public – again in a cynical bid to keep the numbers living longer down.

Sounds incredible but who knows? Those too quick to rule out this admittedly outrageous possibility might rue the day they did.

Certain people claim just as fiercely there's enough space, food sources and free alternative energy supplies to accommodate humanity indefinitely. I tend to think they're right.

But I don't really know one way or the other. Do you? If so, how? Are you really that sure? Or just keeping fingers crossed in a blinkered state of denial?

Leaving the decidedly scary and unbelievable allegations of an impending cull to one side for a moment, when it comes to population growth or environmental damage, the smug and selfish would simply respond "why should I care? – I'm okay and I'll be long gone before it reaches a critical point."

True – but what about future generations? If the forecasts are true, they'll demand to know why something wasn't done. Our apathy could be issuing a lot of them death sentences.

Politicians the world over should be addressing population growth and pressing energy and environmental issues as a matter of urgency. The future of humanity might depend on it.

May 14 – Happy third birthday to my gorgeous granddaughter Chloe. I'm off to Ferndown later for her party at Phil and Emily's – the house they've taken over from her parents, although Gail and Keith still live there too.

It's also my very good friend Carole Jones' daughter Leesa's birthday – so best wishes to her too.

It would have been my dear pal Theresa Bevis' birthday had she not passed away earlier this year aged only 50. I've lit a candle and put a tribute on Facebook to her.

On the music front I've been playing UB40. I'm hoping to see them in concert in October when they come to the O2 Academy in Boscombe. Their gig I saw at Poole on the Present Arms tour in 1981 is one of the best shows I've ever see – and I've seen some total legends!

May 14, evening – Chloe's party was a triumph. Loads of family and friends turned up and it was great to have a catch up with them and see all three of my grandchildren – Chloe, Harvey and Lucas, who was there for the day.

And on that very happy note I shall bring this latest instalment of *Sunshine and Ice* to a close.

****

CHAPTER SEVEN – HIGHER FREQUENCIES

May 15 – The whole reality on which our world is built appears to comprise solid matter. In fact it's nothing of the kind but a whole range of frequencies. Atoms are largely open space and our physical, five-sense aspect is merely a low frequency – Albeit a very convincing one.

If I fell from a first-floor window on to concrete, it would hurt. But that's down to millennia of fierce programming ingrained into the human psyche. Mystics can transcend this.

Spiritually-minded promoters of the light, positive vibration (frequency) try to raise the level while those driven by the darker, more negative energy attempt to lower it.

Religions paint this as the battle between good and evil, God and Satan.

Both currents – positive and negative – constantly battle within us all for supremacy. The negative often seems to be winning the fight and people with the most power appear the most eager to keep it that way or even increase its influence to a point it obliterates the light force.

Why? – Because they're scared that to permit the positive to gain strength would mean they would lose control over us. Power thrives on division. That's how messed up the system is.

People the world over have more in common with each other than they do with those ruling over us all. But as more individuals realize this and find common cause with others similarly waking up, the more this threatens these jittery overlords.

Hence their brutal attempts to intensify divisions and conflict. Free thinkers with open minds are a pain in the arse because they're much harder to control.

Unimaginative, apathetic slaves to the system are, by contrast, a piece of cake.

For my part, I see myself as an advocate for the vibration that brings love, harmony and peace – not hate, discord and war.

And I'm convinced it will triumph in the end. There might well be disruption, chaos, pain and misery along the way, but love will win the day – if enough people want it to.

The tide is turning as humanity faces a leap in its spiritual evolution during the approaching Age of Aquarius.

And on that optimistic note I shall end this twelfth volume of my haphazard, oddball life journal. I hope I've given you food for thought.

Cheerio – M. M.
May 15, 2016

****

If you have to fight to win someone back, they clearly don't think enough of you to warrant it.

Lovers come and go but a true best friend is for keeps.

People are in your life for a reason – but not always the one you think.

I find that writing lyrics is an excellent and relatively harmless way of getting deep hurt, anger and bitterness out of my system.

For my money, the plural of genius is Beatles.

Rock and roll isn't so much a style of music as a state of mind.

Science linked to mysticism can spark light and hope, while technology lacking spirituality poses serious threats to us all.

This book is written in fond memory of Theresa Bevis, one of the closest and most adored and respected friends I ever made in this crazy world. It was an honour.

Also my son John, my Mum and Dad, my sister Jan and all my relatives who have passed over to the other side.

Plus others who have gone the same way – Andy, Umo, Lee, Celtic Nicky, Hairy Pete, Mike Hannen, Samantha, Tarrant and Canadian Mike.

It is dedicated to Phil, Emily, Chloe, Lucas and Harvey. Carol, David, the rest of my rellies and our "adopted" sister Suzette.

To Joe, Paula and Dawn – those extra-special women in my higgledy-piggledy life.

To Kerry, Carole, Sam & Carl, Jem, "Bricktop" Tina, Matt, Tom & Chris, Tina & Jeff, Debs & Al, John P, John G and others who have again proved such good mates.

And to every single one of my chums, colleagues, drinking partners and party pals who have provided me with such brilliant company and sustenance over the years.

Thank you all so very much for the love, laughs, care and support. Yes, there have been hassles, sadness and tears but I've still had a ball!

Keep spreading that love peeps, Martin Money

Author's photo by Sam Excell

www.ingramcontent.com/pod-product-compliance
Lightning Source LLC
Chambersburg PA
CBHW031123250726
48655CB00004B/1819